THE CALIFORNIA WINE COUNTRY COOK BOOK

Compiled and Edited
by
Robert & Virginia Hoffman

Cover:
"California Vineyard"
By Ellie Marshall

Printed in the United States of America

ISBN# 0-9629927-4-7

LIBRARY OF CONGRESS
Catalog Card No. 91-73229

1st Printing—July 17, 1991
2nd Printing—October 18, 1991

Table of Contents

The California Wine Country,
And How it Was Born

The California Wine Country was born in the late 1700s when Father Junipero Serra, a Catholic missionary priest, and his men built and settled a band of missions which ranged from San Diego north to Sonoma, sixty miles north of San Francisco. Requiring wine for the church masses, the missions had brought grapevine stock from Mexico (which came to be known as the Mission Variety Grape) and began making sacramental wine.

As the communities around the missions grew, there developed a market for wine and brandy by the settlers. Soon, as word spread to Europe of the wonderful soil and climate of California, ideal for the growing of wine grapes, vintners emigrated from France, Italy, Switzerland, Germany and Spain, bringing with them grapevine stock of the grapes with which they were familiar.

The Buena Vista Winery, built in 1857, in the town of Sonoma, site of the northernmost mission in California, is considered to be the oldest premium winery in California. The cellars, dug into a limestone hill, are still in use, and are open to visitors daily.

Most of these varieties took to their new home very well, developing slightly different flavors and bouquets, reflecting the soil and climactic conditions. These then became, "California Burgundy," "California Gamay," etc.

It was not until the completion of the transcontinental railroad in the late 1800s that the market for the wines of the state was expanded eastward to the Atlantic seaboard. They did not receive an enthusiastic reception. The East was accustomed to the wines of Europe and these "western wines" made very slow progress in penetrating the eastern market. It was not until California wines won gold medals at prestigious wine tastings in Europe, did these wines win the acceptance of the eastern seaboard. Soon, the wines of California became as acceptable to the American public as American brewed beer.

The ratification of the Volstead Act by Congress, in October of 1919, resulting in the enforcement of Prohibition throughout the United States, was devastating to the burgeoning wine industry of California. The great majority of the vineyards and wineries closed down overnight. A few, believing that the Volstead Act would be repealed, struggled along, making sacramental wine ... but many vineyards were ploughed up and planted to other crops, or simply abandoned and left to grow wild.

Wineries sold their equipment for scrap metal, in many cases, and fine oak barrels handcrafted in France for aging were cut up and sold for firewood.

When this law was repealed in 1934, the few wineries that did remain, rejoiced in the return of their market, but it was not to be for some time. The American public ... an entire generation ... had lost its taste or never acquired a taste for wine. For a considerable period, after Repeal, the only wines that commanded any market in the United States were sweet dessert wines and brandy. Since then, America has learned to relish wine in its many roles: As the perfect accompaniment to food, as an aperitif, as a refreshing drink with minimal calories, and as an important ingredient in the preparation of food.

Today, in the 1990s, more than thirty two different varieties of wine grapes cover more than 300,000 acres of California hills and valleys, with 700 wineries ranging from the family owned and operated wineries that produce a few hundred cases a year to the giants of the industry that produce millions of cases each year.

Whether your preference is the jug table wine or the aged wine, you will find it here in the California Wine Country ... and we hope that these recipes, gathered from those of us who live here, gives you the same pleasure in making these dishes as it did for us to bring them to you.

Contributors

*OUR APPRECIATION TO THE CHEFS,
WINEMAKERS, AND THE WINERIES FOR
SHARING SOME OF THEIR RECIPES WITH US.*

ADLER FELS WINERY
Ayn Ryan Coleman, Co-Owner

BANDIERA WINERY

BELVEDERE WINERY
Gail Paquette, In-House Chef

BENZIGER OF GLEN ELLEN
Stella Fleming, Executive Chef

BOUCHAINE VINEYARDS

BUENA VISTA-CARNEROS ESTATE WINERY
Jill Davis, Winemaker

DUANE BUE
Gourmet Chef

CASWELL WINTER CREEK FARM & VINEYARDS
Helen Caswell, Owner

CHARLES KRUG WINERY
Charlotte Walker, Consultant Chef

CHALK HILL WINERY

CHALONE WINE GROUP
Shirley Sarvis, Consulting Chef

CHATEAU MONTELENA WINERY

CHATEAU SOUVERAIN
Patricia Windisch, Executive Chef and Manager,
Chateau Souverain Restaurant

CLOS DU VAL
Mrs. Bernard Portet

CLOS PEGASE
Mrs. Mitsuko Shrem

DE LOACH VINEYARDS
Christine De Loach

DOMAINE CHANDON
Phillippe Jeanty, Chef de Cuisine

EAGLE RIDGE WINERY OF PENNGROVE
Barry C. Lawrence, Owner & Winemaster

FERRARI-CARANO VINEYARDS & WINERY
Rhonda Carano, Co-Owner

FISHER VINEYARDS
Juelle Fisher, Co-Owner

FICKLIN VINEYARDS
Shirley Sarvis, Consulting Chef

FRANCISCAN VINEYARDS

FREEMARK ABBEY VINEYARDS
Sandra Learned, Consulting Chef

FROG'S LEAP WINERY
Beverly Salinger, Resident Chef

GAN EDEN WINES
Frances R. Winchell

GEYSER PEAK WINERY
Barbara Hom & Anne Vercelli, Chefs

GLORIA FERRER CHAMPAGNE CAVES

GRAND CRU VINEYARDS
Bettina Dreyer, Vice President

GRIST MILL INN
Steven Bennet-Welch

JADED PALATE CATERING CO.
Michele Anna Jordan, Owner

JEKEL VINEYARDS
Donna Wegener, Chef de Cuisine

KENWOOD VINEYARDS
Donna Kilgore, Winery Chef

KORBELL CHAMPAGNE CELLARS

KOZLOWSKI FARMS
Carol Kozlowski-Every and Carmen Kozlowski

LYETH VINEYARDS
Donna Wegener, Chef de Cuisine

LOUIS M. MARTINI WINERY
The Martini Kitchens

MAGLIULO'S RESTAURANT & PENSIONE

MARTINELLI VINEYARDS
Julie Martinelli

MARTINI & PRATI WINES, INC.
Jeani Martini

MATANZAS CREEK WINERY
Christina May Evans, Chef

J.W. MORRIS WINERY
Christina Tate

NAPA BEAUCANON WINERY

PINE RIDGE WINERY
Nancy Andrus, Co-Owner

QUAIL RIDGE CELLARS & VINEYARDS
Elaine Wellesley, Winemaker

RISTORANTI PIATTI
Doug Lane

RODNEY STRONG VINEYARDS
Lucy Cafaro

SAUSAL WINERY
Roselee Demostene and Cindy Martin, Co-Owners

ST. SUPÉRY VINEYARDS & WINERY

SCHRAMSBERG VINEYARDS & CELLARS
Jamie Davies, Co-Owner

SEA RIDGE WINERY
Dee Wickham

SEBASTIANI VINEYARDS
Sylvia Sebastiani

SIMI WINERY
Mary Evely, Chef

SONOMA CHEESE FACTORY

SONOMA VALLEY CUISINE SOCIETY
Keith Fillepello and Early Le Claire,
Consulting Chefs

SONOMA VALLEY VINTNERS ASSOCIATION

STAG'S LEAP WINE CELLARS
Barbara Winiarski, Co-Owner

STERLING VINEYARDS
Richard Alexei, Food & Wine Consultant

SUTTER HOME WINERY
Winners National Burger Contest

TIMBERCREST FARMS
The Waltenspiel Kitchens

WM. WHEELER WINERY
Ingrid Wheeler, Co-Owner

WILLETTS BREWING CO.
Stephen Meyer, Chef

Cooking With Wine,
Some Guidelines that May Help You

The most important guide in choosing which wine to use as an ingredient in which food ... is you. Try some of the guidelines that we have noted here ... and then, based upon that, broaden your range by trying different wines in different proportions in different dishes. But ... remember a few things. The first is to taste the wine you are going to use in cooking. If it tastes good ... use it. If you don't like the taste ... don't use it. Cooking will not hide the taste that you don't like: it will intensify it. Second, the price of the wine does not make it, necessarily, a great wine for cooking. Great subtleties in bouquets and multiple flavors are sometimes diminished when subjected to heat with herbs, spices, etc. Remember, too, that wine as an ingredient in cooking is meant to enhance the dish ... not to dominate it.

	WINE	QUANTITY
SOUPS		
Cream, Clear	Dry Sherry	1 teaspoon per portion
Vegetable, Meat	Red, White	1 teaspoon per portion
MEATS		
Beef	Red, Brandy	1/4 cup per pound
Lamb, Veal	White	1/4 cup per pound
Ham, Baked	White, Port	2 cups (baste)
Kidneys, Brains, etc.	White	1/4 cup per pound
PASTAS		
Tomato Sauce	Red	1/4 cup per portion
Cream Sauce	White	1/4 cup per portion
POULTRY		
Chicken, roasted	White	1/2 cup per pound (baste)
Chicken, poached	White	1/2 cup per pound
Turkey, roasted	White, Red	1/2 cup per pound (baste)
Cornish Game Hen	White, Red	1/4 cup per pound (baste)
Duck	Red, Brandy	1/4 cup per pound (baste)

	WINE	QUANTITY
SEAFOOD		
Fish, broiled	Dry White	1/4 cup per pound
Fish, poached	Dry White	1/4 cup per pound
Fish, baked	Dry White	1/4 cup per pound
Fish, sauteed	Dry White	4 tablespoons per pound
Shellfish	Dry White	1/4 cup per pound
FRUITS & VEGETABLES		
Fresh Fruit	Champagne, White	To taste
Cooked Vegetables	Dry White	To taste
Salads	White, Red	To taste

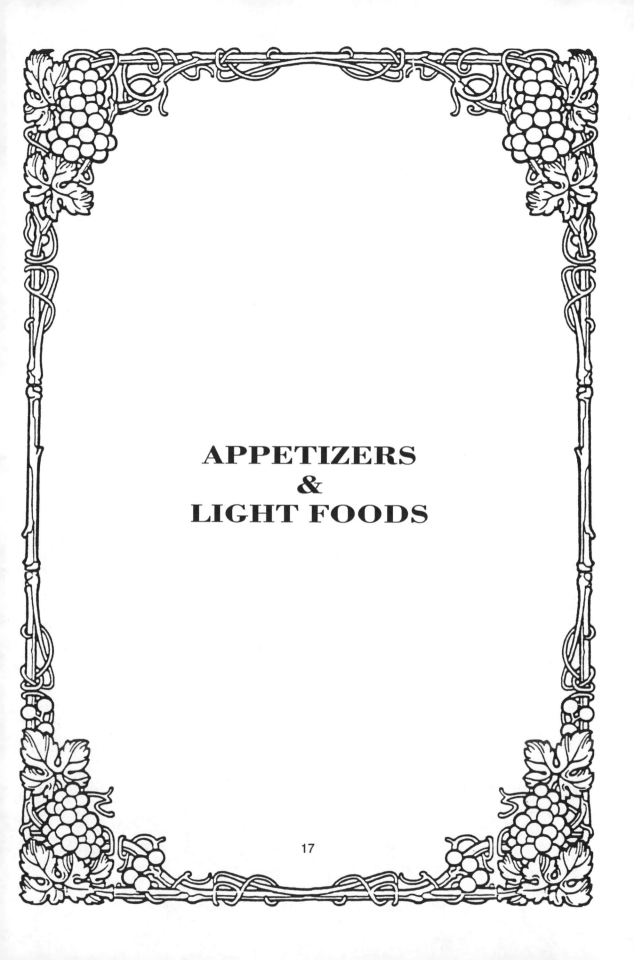

APPETIZERS
&
LIGHT FOODS

Crostini with Goat Cheese,
Sun Dried Tomatoes and a Basil Leaf

4 medium sun-dried tomato
  halves in oil
2 tablespoons oil from the
  tomatoes (or olive oil)

8 ounces young goat cheese
fresh basil leaves
32 crostini (below)

Combine the sun-dried tomatoes, oil and goat cheese in a food processor and puree. The mixture will be a brilliant pink color. There should be no large pieces of tomato remaining. The mixture can be prepared in advance and refrigerated for several days. On each crostini place a small basil leaf (or half of a large one) on one side. Smear a dollop of the goat cheese on the other side, coming half-way up the leaf. You can pipe the cheese on decoratively with a forcing bag if you want to be more formal. These hold very well and you can assemble them 1/2 hour in advance.

CROSTINI:

French bread baguette
4 tablespoons olive oil

Slice the baguette 1/8-1/4 inch thick. Brush the slices lightly with olive oil. Arrange on a baking sheet and toast in a 425° oven until nicely browned. When cool, they should be totally dry and crisp. Return any that are moist to a hot oven for another minute. These crostini can be made well in advance, even stored airtight for several days. If they get limp from humidity, a few seconds in a hot oven will recrisp them.

I suggest Sterling Vineyards 1989 Sauvignon Blanc to accompany this dish.

Richard Alexei
Food & Wine Consultant, Sterling Vineyards

Smoked Salmon Flan

pastry for 9 inch pie
1 cup cream
1 cup milk
4 whole eggs
ground white pepper

1/2 cup grated Swiss or Gruyere
cheese
1 cup chopped smoked
salmon
pinch nutmeg

Preheat oven to 375°. Line a 9 inch pie pan with rich pastry dough. Prick well and bake 5 minutes. Meanwhile, beat 4 eggs, add milk, cream and cheese. Stir in smoked salmon and spices. Pour into prepared crust and bake 30 to 35 minutes. Serves 6 to 8.

Serve with our Schramsberg Reserve.

Jamie Davies, Co-Owner
Schramsberg Vineyards and Cellars

Lahmajoon

1 pound lamb shoulder, ground fine
2 cups onion, chopped fine
1/4 cup parsley, chopped
1/2 small green pepper, chopped

1/2 clove garlic, chopped
(optional)
6 ounce can tomato paste
1/2 small can whole tomatoes,
drained

Mix ingredients together and spread onto ready made pizza dough or flour tortillas. Serves 8-10.

Ayn Ryan Coleman, Co-Owner
Adler Fels Winery

Another interesting Armenian recipe from Ayn Rand Coleman. Traditionally served as an appetizer similar to pizza.

Smoked Salmon Cheesecake

2 tablespoons butter
1 cup chopped onion
16 ounces cream cheese
8 ounces goat cheese
1/2 cup grated Parmesan

4 large eggs
1/3 cup half & half
1/2 pound smoked salmon
  trimmings

Butter 8-inch springform pan. Set oven to 300°. In saucepan melt butter and add onion, saute until tender, set aside to cool. In food processor, mix cheeses, eggs, smoked salmon and half & half. Blend until smooth. Stir in onions. Pour mixture into pan. Bake until firm, about 1 hour. Chill for one hour. Serve with water biscuits.

Our Matanzas Creek Chardonnay accompanies this perfectly.

Christina May Evans, Chef
Matanzas Creek Winery

Savory Shortbread

2 cups flour, sifted
1 teaspoon sea salt
1/4 cup sweet butter, very cold

3 ounces blue cheese, very cold
3 eggs, lightly beaten

Preheat the oven to 400°. Combine the flour and salt in a food processor fitted with a steel blade. Pulse briefly to combine. Add the cold butter, cheese and eggs and process until a soft dough forms. With lightly floured hands, pat the dough into a 8-10 inch square. Place the dough on a well-buttered baking pan and cut into bite size pieces. Bake until lightly browned. Cool before serving. (Can be stored for two weeks in an airtight container.)

Donna Kilgore, Winery Chef
Kenwood Vineyards

Sonoma Goat Cheese Torta

1 pound mild goat cheese (cream
   cheese may be substituted)
1/2 pound unsalted butter
6 ounces sun-dried tomatoes
   packed in oil, drained
2 cups basil, firmly packed

4 cloves of garlic
1/2 teaspoon salt
1/2 teaspoon pepper
1/3 cup olive oil
plastic wrap

In a food processor combine goat cheese and butter until well blended, set aside. In food processor, chop sun-dried tomatoes, set aside. In food processor, place basil, garlic, salt and pepper. With motor running, slowly drizzle in the oil through the feed tube, and process until the basil is pureed, set aside. Line 3 cup mold or loaf pan with plastic wrap. Spread 1/3 of goat cheese mixture in bottom of the mold. Spread with 1/2 cup of basil mixture. Top with another 1/3 of goat cheese mixture. Spread with sun-dried tomatoes. Top with remaining goat cheese. Refrigerate until firm, at least 1 hour. To serve, unmold onto plate and spread on crackers or toasted garlic croutons (slices of baguettes oven toasted with garlic butter). Serves 8.

You'll enjoy Benziger of Glen Ellen Cabernet Sauvignon with this.

Stella Fleming, Executive Chef
Benziger of Glen Ellen Winery

Black Forest Ham Appetizer

12 thin slices Black Forest ham
12 carrot sticks 2x1/4 inches
8 ounces cream cheese
1/2 teaspoon salt
a dash of Tabasco

12 celery sticks 2x1/4 inches
1 bunch scallions, diced
1/2 red pepper, finely diced
1/2 teaspoon pepper
a dash of Worcestershire sauce

Cut ham slices in half. Prepare celery and carrot sticks. Let cream cheese soften to room temperature. Mix cream cheese with pepper and scallions. Add seasoning. Spread on ham. Place celery stick in middle and roll up. Repeat same procedure with carrot stick.

Serve with Lyeth Alexander Valley white wine.

Donna Wegener, Chef de Cuisine
Lyeth Winery

Feta Cheese and Chive Spread

8 ounces cream cheese at
  room temperature
6 ounces feta cheese
2 anchovy filets
4 ounces sweet butter at
  room temperature

1/4 cup sour cream
1 garlic clove, crushed
2 tablespoons minced chives
4-8 drops hot red pepper sauce
Greek olives for garnish

Cover feta cheese in cold water and soak for 10 minutes, changing water once. Drain. Blend cheese, anchovy, butter, and sour cream until smooth, Stir in garlic, chives, and hot pepper sauce. Spread on toast points, croutons or crackers and garnish with Greek olive wedges.

A creamy flavorful appetizer to accompany our barrel fermented Chardonnay.

Elaine Wellesley, Winemaker
Quail Ridge Cellars & Vineyards

Marinated Salmon with Dill Mayonnaise

8 ounce salmon fillet
1 teaspoon lemon juice
2 tablespoons fresh dill, chopped
1 tablespoon olive oil

6 thinly sliced radishes
1/4 English cucumber, thinly
  sliced
capers

Cut salmon across grain into 1/4 inch slices. Place each slice on individual plastic wrap and rub with oil and lemon juice and sprinkle with fresh dill. Pound until half its original thickness. Refrigerate in plastic wrap for at least 8 hours. Unwrap and serve with toasted slices of thinly wholegrain bread, radishes, cucumber, capers and dill mayonnaise.

DILL MAYONNAISE:

2 egg yolks
1/2 teaspoon Dijon mustard
white wine vinegar

1 cup olive oil
1/4 cup chopped fresh dill
1 teaspoon sugar

Mix egg yolks, mustard and 1/2 teaspoon white wine vinegar in food processor. Slowly add 1/2 cup olive oil, blend until thickened. Add 1 tablespoon wine vinegar. Slowly add remaining 1/2 cup olive oil and 1 teaspoon sugar, blend. Stir in dill.

The wine: Matanzas Creek Sauvignon Blanc.

Christina May Evans, Chef
Matanzas Creek Winery

Corn Griddle-Cakes
with Avocado and Smoked Chicken

1/2 cup corn kernels
  (fresh or frozen)
1/2 cup cornmeal
1/2 cup boiling water
1/2 cup flour
1/2 teaspoon salt

2 teaspoons baking powder
1 egg
1/2 cup milk
2 ounces butter, melted
butter for cooking

Puree the corn kernels in a food processor or chop well with a knife then mash with a wooden spoon. Combine cornmeal and boiling water and stir until water is absorbed. Add pureed corn, flour, salt and baking powder and milk and whisk. Add egg and butter and whisk just until all ingredients are well combined. The batter may be made up to an hour in advance.

Heat a large skillet or griddle and brush with melted butter. Pour about 1 tablespoon of batter or each - remember they're finger-food so keep them small. When the top begins to solidify, flip the cake (a narrow, flexible blade spatula is best for this). Adjust heat so that both sides brown nicely. Transfer to a warm oven and continue until all batter is used. Yield: about 36 griddle cakes 1 1/2 inches in diameter.

SMOKED CHICKEN:

2 cups chopped smoked chicken
1 tablespoon mayonnaise
2 teaspoons dijon mustard

Note: Smoked chickens are widely available in meat markets, delicatessens and specialty shops. If not obtainable, smoked turkey breast is the closest substitute.

Combine chicken, mustard and mayonnaise. Should your smoked chicken be dry, a little more mayonnaise may be necessary. This can be prepared in advance and refrigerated but let it warm a little before using.

AVOCADO:

2 medium ripe Haas avocados
lemon

Cut the avocadoes in half, remove the pit and scoop out the flesh with a spoon. In a bowl, mash the avocados and a few drops of lemon juice with a fork. It should be a little lumpy. Do not add salt since this component is meant to balance the saltiness of smoked chicken. Place a piece of plastic wrap directly on the avocado puree to keep it from darkening. It's best not to mash the avocados more than an hour or two in advance.

TO ASSEMBLE:

Spread each warm griddle-cake with a teaspoon of the avocado, then top with a tablespoon of the smoked chicken. A tiny parsley leaf can garnish each.

This tasty hors d'oeuvre offers an unusual and delightful combination of flavors and textures.

1988 Sterling Vineyards' Lake Chardonnay accompanies this dish.

Richard Alexie, Food & Wine Consultant
Sterling Vineyards

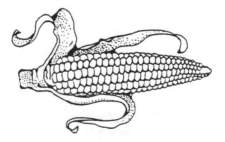

Japanese Ahi Tostados

4 Ahi (tuna) steaks
soy sauce
4 tomatoes, peeled, seeded &
  diced
4 fresh shiso leaves, chopped*
won ton skins
cream fraiche

slivered ginger
sesame oil
2 cloves minced garlic
2 chopped green onions
2 teaspoons rice wine vinegar
wasabi*

Combine soy sauce, slivered ginger and sesame oil and marinate tuna steaks. Combine tomatoes, shiso leaves, green onions, garlic and rice wine vinegar, set aside. Mix a little water with wasabi to form a soft paste. Fry won ton skins in hot oil until crisp and golden. Sear the tuna steaks in hot pan, 30 seconds on each side. The tuna should be raw in the center. Slice in 1/8 inch thick strips.

Place a strip of tuna on a won ton and spread a little bit of wasabi paste on it (very little as it would tend to overpower any wine). Top with a spoonful of tomato salsa. Garnish with a little creme fraiche and green onions.

To be served with Geyser Peak Sauvignon Blanc.

*Available in Japanese markets.

Barbara Hom, Chef
Geyser Peak Winery

This recipe was a Silver Medal winner at Sonoma County Harvest Fair.

Smoked Trout with Ancho Chili Mayonnaise

1 smoked trout, about 1/2 pound
8 to 10 ancho chilies
1 cup mayonnaise

Put chilies in a bowl, cover with warm water and soak overnight. The next day remove seeds and stems and puree in food processor. Rub through a sieve and reserve. Add chili puree to one cup good mayonnaise (preferably homemade) and allow the flavors to blend for at least a day. Spread mayonnaise on thinly sliced, toasted baguette. Top with "chevron" of smoked trout. Garnish with fresh herbs. Serves 6 to 8.

Serve with our Schramsberg Crémant.

Jamie Davies, Co-Owner
Schramsberg Vineyards and Cellars

Hot Crab Dip

4 6-ounce cans crabmeat
1/2 cup onion, minced
1 tablespoon jalapeno mustard
1/4 cup Chardonnay.

1 cup mayonnaise
2 tablespoons lemon juice
8 ounces cream cheese, softened

Beat cream cheese until smooth. Add crabmeat (2 cans drained, 2 cans with juice). Add 1/4 cup Chardonnay. Cook in greased ovenproof dish at 350° for 30 minutes. Makes 3 cups. Serve with crackers or French bread. Good warm or cold. Serves 10.

Serve with Martinelli's Chardonnay.

Julie Martinelli
Martinelli Vineyards

Prosciutto and Mushroom Bread

1/4 pound prosciutto, thick slices, diced
3/4 cup Sauvignon Blanc
8 ounces shallots, peeled & chopped
2 cloves garlic, minced
6 tablespoons sweet butter
olive oil

2 pounds mushrooms*
1 cup Italian parsley, chopped
3 tablespoons fresh thyme, chopped
salt and pepper to taste
1 large loaf sourdough French bread

Preheat oven to 350°. In a small pan, cook the prosciutto in 2 tablespoons of butter until crisp. Remove the proscuitto and reserve. Deglaze the pan with the 3/4 cup Sauvignon Blanc and set aside. In a large saute pan, saute the onion and garlic in 4 tablespoons butter until transparent, approximately 15 minutes over low heat. Add the mushrooms, parsley, thyme, salt and pepper. Cook until the mushrooms have released their liquid and the mixture is almost dry. Add the proscuitto and Sauvignon Blanc.

Cook over medium heat until the wine is reduced to 2 tablespoons. Set aside to cool. Slice the bread in half and remove the soft interior, leaving 1/2 inch thickness of bread on the crust surface. Fill the loaf with the prosciutto/mushroom mixture. Replace the top of the loaf and brush the crust with olive oil. Place on a cookie sheet and bake for 20 minutes. May be served hot or at room temperature. Slice just before serving. Makes 12 servings.

*Combination of shiitake, chanterelle, and oyster, cleaned and sliced.

Suggested wine: Kenwood Sauvignon Blanc.

Donna Kilgore,
Kenwood Vineyards

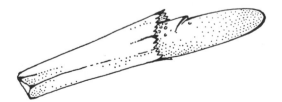

Mushrooms a la Gloria

6 tablespoons butter, room
  temperature
1 tablespoon minced garlic
1 1/2 pounds mushrooms, cleaned
  stemmed

1 1/2 cups Brut sparkling wine
salt and pepper to taste
1 to 2 tablespoons minced fresh
  parsley or mixed fresh herbs

In 10-inch skillet, melt 3 tablespoons of the butter over medium heat; add garlic. Cook and stir garlic until lightly browned, add mushrooms. Cook, stirring occasionally, until lightly browned, about 5 minutes. Add Brut, bring to boil. Reduce heat, simmer until liquid is reduced to 1/3 cup, about 10 minutes. Taste and adjust seasoning with salt and pepper. Remove from heat; whisk in remaining butter until sauce is slightly thickened. Arrange mushrooms in serving dish with toothpick inserted in each. Pour sauce over; garnish with minced parsley or fresh herbs. Serves 6.

Gloria Ferrer Brut (NV) is suggested.

From Gloria Ferrer Champagne Caves

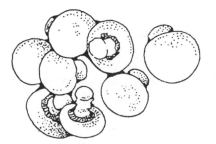

Eggplant Pizzetas

3 eggplants, sliced crossway
10 cloves garlic, peeled and
  chopped fine
pizza dough
tomato sauce

1 cup olive oil
salt
1 pound mozzarella, thinly
  sliced or grated

Place sliced eggplant onto a sheet pan and sprinkle with salt. Let stand 20 minutes. Turn slices over and repeat process. Pat each slice dry with paper towel. Heat enough olive oil in a large skillet to cover the bottom. Over medium heat saute eggplant and part of the garlic. Cook until golden brown and wilted. Set aside to cool. Repeat process until all the eggplant is cooked.

Spread a spoonful of tomato sauce on partially cooked pizza dough. Place eggplant over tomato sauce and finish by placing a liberal amount of cheese on top. Bake at 400° until piping hot and cheese is melted and golden brown on top. Serve immediately. 24 pizzetas.

PIZZA DOUGH:

1 1/2 ounces dry yeast
6 cups warm water
7 cups all purpose flour
cornmeal

4 ounces milk
2 tablespoons salt
5 pounds flour

Combine the yeast, 2 cups of water, 2 cups of flour with a whisk to make a thin pasty liquid. Let stand in a warm part of the kitchen for 20 minutes to make a frothy "sponge." Place sponge, oil, milk, rest of water and salt in mixer and knead while adding rest of flour. Add enough flour to form a soft dough that comes together and clings to the side of the bowl. Knead approximately 10 minutes. If making by hand, place about half the flour on bread board. Make a well and put in the rest of the ingredients. Gently mix ingredients together, adding more flour and kneading to form a soft elastic dough. Knead approximately 10 minutes after all the flour is added. Place the dough in a well-oiled bowl.

Cover and place in a warm place and let the dough rise until double in size (about 2 hours). Punch the dough down and let rise again. Turn dough out onto floured board and cut desired size. Roll dough out to about 1/4 inch thickness.

Oil sheet pan and sprinkle with a little cornmeal. Place dough on pan and brush lightly with olive oil. Let rest approximately 30 minutes. Preheat oven to 400° then bake until golden. Remove from oven and let cool.

TOMATO SAUCE:

5 pounds fresh plum tomatoes,   1/4 cup olive oil
    peeled, seeded and chopped   2 teaspoons dried oregano
    or 4 cans plum tomatoes,   salt and pepper to taste
    drained and chopped

Saute tomatoes in oil with spices over medium heat for 5 minutes. Place in food processor and blend. Strain and add more oregano if desired.

Great with Frog's Leap Zinfandel or Chardonnay.

Beverly Salinger, Resident Chef
Frog's Leap Winery

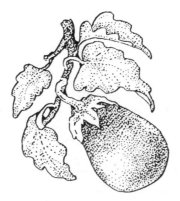

Pizzalinas

Pizzalinas are mini-pizzas, great for cocktail parties or everyday snacks. You begin with a great meaty, wine-tomato sauce (see recipe below). Spread it on French bread baguettes sliced about 1/4" thick, sprinkle Parmesan cheese and oregano on the top and bake on a cookie sheet until bubbly (about 25 minutes in a slow oven). Serve piping hot.

SAUCE:

1 medium can tomato sauce
1 medium can tomato paste
1/4 cup Zinfandel
1 small can sliced mushrooms
salt and pepper to taste

1 medium chopped onion
1 pound ground beef
1 tablespoon olive oil
2 garlic cloves

Brown the ground beef in the olive oil and stir in the garlic and onion. Add tomato sauce, tomato paste and Zinfandel and bring to a boil. Stir in the mushrooms; add salt and pepper to taste. Let simmer until sauce is thick. Serves 8.

Serve with Sausal Zinfandel

Roselee Demostene & Cindy Martin, Co-Owners
Sausal Winery

Olive Oil Dolma

1 large bottle grape leaves
6 large onions, chopped finely
1 1/2 cup olive oil
salt to taste
1 tomato, chopped fine and
  juice squeezed out

1/3 cup lemon juice (or to taste)
1/3 cup parsley, chopped fine
1 teaspoon Cayenne (or to taste)
2 cups rice

Place 1 cup olive oil in large fry pan. Add onions and cook until onions have a clear look. Add remaining ingredients and cook until all of the liquid is gone. Taste for more seasoning. (We like ours spicy.) Remove from stove and cool. Rinse leaves a little and squeeze dry. Pinch off stems and place in bottom of large heavy pan.

Place leaf open (with smooth side down) in your hand or on dish. Place 1 teaspoonful at the top of leaf. Fold sides over and roll to end. Place, seam side down, in pan. Continue until all are rolled. Save fine leaves to place on top of rolls to keep them from turning dark. Mix 2 cups water with 1/2 cup olive oil and gently pour over top. Place a heavy plate on top of leaves (to keep them from moving) and then the lid. Bake for 1 hour and 20 minutes or until water is absorbed in a 350° oven.

Remove from oven and check to see if rice is cooked. Cool. These can be refrigerated for days. If refrigerated, it is important to remove dolma from refrigerator 1 hour before serving. Remove and arrange on large platter with sprigs of parsley and lemon if desired. Cover until ready to serve. Serves 12.

We have served this as an appetizer or first course at Adler Fels. It is a favorite of our guests.

Serve with Adler Fels Sobra Vista Chardonnay.

By Ayn Ryan Coleman, Co-Owner
Alder Fels Vineyards

Focaccia with Caramelized Onions

1 loaf (1 pound) frozen bread
dough, thawed as package directs
1 jar (8 ounces) Sonoma marinated
dried tomatoes, drained
(reserve oil)
2/3 cup freshly grated Parmesan
cheese

3 cups sliced onions
1/4 teaspoon salt
2 tablespoons chopped fresh
rosemary leaves or 2 teaspoons
dried rosemary, crumbled

Oil a 9x13 inch baking pan. Roll and stretch dough on lightly floured surface; fit into oil pan. Cover with plastic wrap and set aside in warm place until doubled, about 45 minutes. Meanwhile, in large skillet combine 2 tablespoons of the reserved oil and the onions. Cook over low heat, stirring occasionally, until golden brown, about 30 minutes. Mix in salt and set aside. Brush top of dough with the remaining oil. Cover with the onions and sprinkle with rosemary. Arrange tomatoes on top. Sprinkle with cheese.

Bake in center of preheated 425° oven 35 to 40 minutes until springy to the touch and bread is brown around the edges. During the last 15 minutes cover lightly with foil to prevent over-browning, if necessary. Cut into squares while warm. Makes 12 (3x4 inch) squares. Serves focaccia as an appetizer or as a savory accompaniment to soups and salad.

Waltenspiel's Kitchen
Timber Crest Farms

Grilled Polenta with Fontina Cheese, Shiitake Mushrooms and Sun-Dried Tomatoes

4 cups water
1 cup polenta or yellow corn meal
1 tablespoon minced fresh parsley
1/2 cup green onions, minced
1/2 cup mushrooms, minced
salt and pepper
1/4 pound Fontina cheese, thinly
  sliced

1/2 cup dry white wine
1/4 pound (1 stick) butter
2 teaspoons ground white pepper
1 teaspoon fresh thyme or
  oregano (use 1/2 if using dry
  herbs)
shiitake mushrooms & sun-dried
  tomatoes for garnish

Bring water, salt, pepper and thyme to a boil in large saucepan. Slowly beat in polenta with a whisk to avoid lumps. Reduce heat to low and stir to prevent sticking. Cook slowly for 10 minutes. In a separate pan, saute mushrooms and green onions in 2 tablespoons of butter until cooked through and just beginning to brown. Season with a little salt and pepper, add wine and reduce until most of the wine cooks away. Add to polenta mixture with remaining butter and parsley.

Off heat, spread polenta mixture on buttered cake pan or cookie sheet so that it is approximately 1/2 inch thick. Cool, cover with plastic and refrigerate up to a day in advance. To complete the dish, cut polenta into diamonds or other interesting shapes.

Grill over mesquite until surface is lightly toasted. Turn, place a slice of fontina cheese on top and allow to just melt. Serve warm, garnished with grilled shiitake mushrooms and slivers of sun-dried tomatoes. Serves 6-8.

Serve with Martini Zinfandel.

Louis M. Martini Winery

Fondue Natural

2 cups grated Gruyere
2 cups grated Fontina
3 tablespoons flour
1/8 teaspoon nutmeg
1/8 teaspoon white pepper

pinch Cayenne
3 cloves garlic
1 1/2 cups Champagne
1/2 teaspoon caraway seeds
1 tablespoon Brandy

Combine grated cheeses, flour, nutmeg, white pepper, and Cayenne. Rub the inside of a saucepan with garlic cloves and set garlic aside. Add Champagne to saucepan and heat to just under a boil. Turn heat down to low and add grated cheese mixture a little at a time, stirring constantly with a wooden spoon. Add garlic cloves and caraway seeds. When fondue is well melted with a smooth consistency, remove garlic cloves, add Brandy and serve with sliced French bread.

Serve with our Korbel Natural Champagne.

F. Korbell & Bros. Inc.
Champagne Cellars

Herbed Scrambled Eggs in Croustades

12 slices homemade-style white
  bread, remove crusts
4 tablespoons melted butter
10 large eggs
1/2 pound sausage of choice
4 scallions, chopped

1/2 teaspoon dry sage
1 teaspoon fresh thyme or 1/2
  teaspoon dry
1 teaspoon fresh tarragon or
  1/2 teaspoon dry
1/4 cup water

Lightly brush bread with 2 tablespoons of melted butter. Press each slice into 1/2 cup muffin pan. Bake in 350° oven for 20 to 25 minutes. While croustades are browning, saute scallions. In a bowl, whisk together eggs, water and herbs. Add to skillet and cook slowly until eggs are creamy. Stir in reserved sausage. Divide eggs into croustades, garnish with herb sprigs and serve. Serves 6.

Serve with our Schramsberg Cuvée de Pinot.

Jamie Davies, Co-Owner
Schramsberg Vineyards and Cellars

A very quick, simple, yet elegant appetizer, or as a main course.

SOUPS

Red Bell Pepper Soup

1 large white onion, peeled and
  chopped
6 large red bell peppers, seeded
  and chopped coarsely
3 tablespoons sweet butter
2 cloves garlic

6 cups chicken stock
1 cup whipping cream
salt and pepper to taste
1/2 lime and 1 tablespoon lime
  zest
sour cream

In a heavy saucepan melt the butter over a medium flame. Add the onions and cook, stirring occasionally until onions are soft and brown. Add the chunks of red bell pepper and stir until the peppers are soft but not burnt or charred. Add the garlic cloves and chicken stock, increase the flame and bring to a boil. Let mixture cook until red bell peppers are completely softened. Approximately 30 minutes. Remove from the stove and puree in batches in blender, food processor. Do not fill blender more than half full to prevent leakage. Return soup puree mixture to new pot, add the cream and bring to a boil. Reduce flame to a simmer and reduce by 1/5 and season to taste with salt and pepper. Add the lime juice. Before serving add a dab of sour cream and the zest of lime to each serving. Serve or let cool and refrigerate. Serves 4.

Serve with Stag's Leap Wine Cellars Napa Valley Chardonnay.

Barbara Winiarski, Co-Owner
Stag's Leap Wine Cellars

Harvest Soup

4 tablespoons butter
1/2 medium onion, minced
2 shallots, minced
1 stalk celery
1 carrot, peeled & minced
1 teaspoon fresh chives
2 cups canned pumpkin
2 teaspoons grated orange
  zest

2 dashes hot red pepper sauce
2 cups chicken broth
1 cup half & half
1/2 cup heavy cream
1/4 cup orange juice
1/4 cup Chardonnay
1 cup sour cream
3/4 teaspoon salt

Heat butter in medium sauce pan over medium heat. Add onions, shallots, celery and carrot. Cook, stirring constantly until softened, about 7 minutes. Stir in pumpkin and chicken broth; simmer uncovered 10 minutes.

Transfer to blender or food processor and puree until smooth. Return to sauce pan. Stir in half & half, cream, orange juice and Chardonnay. Heat until lightly boiling. Reduce heat and simmer uncovered for 10 minutes. Meanwhile, combine sour cream, chives and orange zest in a small bowl. Season soup with salt and red pepper sauce and top each serving with a dollop of sour cream mixture. Serves 6.

Jill Davis, Winemaker
Buena Vista-Carneros Estate

Roasted Japanese Eggplant Soup
with Goat's Milk Mozzarella Croutons

1 1/2 pounds Japanese eggplant
2 medium yellow onions
1 medium sweet red pepper
3 Roma tomatoes
8 cloves garlic, peeled
3 branches thyme, chopped

3 branches basil, chopped
1 bay leaf, crumbled
1 teaspoon unsalted butter
1/4-1/2 cup extra virgin olive oil
2 quarts chicken stock
salt and pepper to taste

Halve the eggplant, lightly coat with olive oil, salt and pepper. Halve the onions lengthwise, cut out the root end and peel down to the last layer of skin. Halve the pepper, remove stem and seed, lightly coat with olive oil and salt and pepper. Remove stem end from the tomatoes. Place all these ingredients on a foil lined sheet pan. Skin side down for the eggplant, cut side down for the onion, skin side up for the pepper.

Place in preheated 400° oven until the eggplant and pepper browns; 20-25 minutes. At about 10 minutes add the garlic cloves. When the eggplant is nicely roasted and the pepper halves are brown and puffy, remove pan from oven. When cool enough to handle, peel the onion and the pepper. Coarsely chop the eggplant, pepper, onion and garlic. It won't be necessary to chop the tomatoes. In an 8 quart pot, melt the butter and add the remaining olive oil. Add the chopped vegetables and herbs. Mix well. Add enough chicken stock to barely cover. Bring to a boil and add the crumbled bay leaf. Let the mix simmer until it starts to thicken. Puree in blender. The resulting puree should be thick and textured, flecked with the black bits of eggplant.

When serving, add chicken stock to base until it has a stew-like consistency. Salt and pepper to taste. Top each portion with goat's milk mozzarella croutons. (Toasted sliced bread with a 1/4" slice of mozzarella on top, melted in the oven.) Preparation time: approximately 1 hour. Serves six.

Chandon Brut makes a perfect accompaniment to this dish.

Philippe Jeanty, Chef de Cuisine
Domaine Chandon

Monastery Lentils
(A Hearty Soup or Supper Dish)

1/4 cup olive oil
2 large onions, chopped
1 carrot, chopped
1/2 teaspoon thyme
1/2 teaspoon marjoram
3 cups stock or seasoned water

1 cup dry lentils, washed
1/4 cup chopped fresh parsley
1 pound canned tomatoes
1/4 cup Cabernet Sauvignon
2/3 cup grated Swiss cheese
2 links Italian sweet or hot
  sausage (optional)

Heat the olive oil in a large saucepan and saute the onions and carrot for 3 to 5 minutes, add the herbs and saute for 1 minute more. Add the stock or water, lentils, parsley and tomatoes with their juice. If sausage is used, cut the links into bite-size chunks, brown lightly under the broiler and add to the lentils. Cover the saucepan and cook until the lentils are tender (45-60 minutes). Add the Cabernet Sauvignon. Taste for seasoning, adding more salt if necessary.

To serve, place 2 tablespoons of grated cheese in each serving bowl and top with soup. This dish is especial delicious served with corn muffins. May be made ahead and reheated - it gets better and better! Serves 4-6.

We suggest Quail Ridge 1986 Napa Valley Cabernet Sauvignon.

Elaine Wellesley, Winemaker
Quail Ridge Cellars & Vineyards

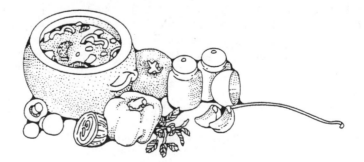

Hearty Spring Vegetable Chowder with Ham

3 strips of chopped bacon
6 cups chicken stock
2 medium sliced brown onions
6 garlic cloves, minced
3 stalks 1/4" sliced celery
3 10" carrots sliced 1/4"
2 large peeled and cubed
  brown potatoes
2 teaspoons cumin
1 teaspoon salt
dash Cayenne

1 1/4 pound cured ham
1 pound broccoli flowerettes
1/2 pound green beans, trimmed
  into thirds
2 medium tomatoes, seeded, cut
  into chunks
8 ounces halved mushrooms
8 1/2 ounces corn (canned or
  fresh), drained
2 tablespoons olive oil

In a large stock pot, cook bacon until brown. Remove bacon pieces, set aside. Add olive oil. Saute onions, garlic, celery until tender, stir approximately 5 minutes. Add potatoes, stir 10 minutes. Add chicken stock. Transfer 1/2 of mixture to food processor, puree until smooth. Return to stock pot. Add remaining vegetables and season with spices. Bring to slow boil. Reduce to simmer, uncovered for approximately 40 minutes or until vegetables are tender. Add ham and bacon bits. Season to taste. Serves 6 to 8.

Jill Davis, Winemaker
Buena Vista-Carneros Estate

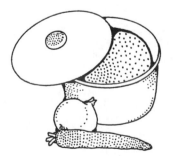

Curried Chicken and Olive Soup

1 2-1/2 or 3 pound broiling chicken
2 large onions, sliced thin
2 large tart apples, sliced
1 can of peas, including liquid
2/3 cup of green stuffed olives,
  chopped
3 cups of milk
2 stalks of celery, cut in pieces

1/2 teaspoon salt
1 teaspoon chili powder
1 teaspoon curry powder
1/2 cup all purpose flour
1/4 pound margarine or butter
1 cup cream
1 medium onion, cut in pieces

Boil chicken in 4 cups of water, with the medium onion pieces and the 2 stalks of celery for approximately one hour until tender. Cool and drain. Strain broth and put aside 3 cups. Dice chicken to total approximately 1 1/2 to 2 cups. Fry the remaining onions and apples in margarine or butter, adding the salt, chili powder, curry powder and flour. Stir well. Now add the chicken broth, and the peas. Cook until tender, stirring frequently. Now add the milk, diced chicken, and chopped olives. Bring to a boil and add cream. Serve hot, immediately. Serves 6 to 8 persons.

A dry white wine is appropriate for this, when served as a main course.

Admittedly a very unusual combination of ingredients, but well worth the effort, resulting in a very, very good soup ... easily a main course when served with a mixed green salad and crusty French bread. VMH

Quick Minestrone

1 11 ounce can red kidney beans
1 teaspoon salt
1/2 teaspoon garlic salt
1 clove garlic, pressed
1/4 teaspoon pepper
1 tablespoon oil
1/4 cup chopped parsley
1 small zucchini, unpeeled and cut
  into small cubes
2 stalks celery, chopped
1 small carrot, diced

2 green onions, chopped
4-5 leaves Swiss chard, chopped
3 tablespoons butter
1 8 ounce can tomato sauce or
  1 can solid pack tomatoes,
  mashed
2 1/4 cups water
1/2 cup Pinot Noir Blanc wine
1/4 cup uncooked elbow
  macaroni (optional)
grated Parmesan cheese

Place undrained beans in a large kettle or saucepan; mash about 2/3 of the beans and leave the rest whole. Add salt, garlic salt, garlic, pepper, oil and parsley, stirring well. Then add all the vegetables, butter, tomato sauce and water. Simmer 1 hour or more and then add wine. (If desired, macaroni may be added at this point.) Simmer 10-15 minutes longer. Sprinkle with cheese before serving. Serves 6. If soup seems too thick add more water and salt to taste.

Minestrone is an old recipe that used to take about half a day to prepare, starting with dry red beans. This is a modern version using canned kidney beans and it is equally as good as the old. I usually serve it with garlic bread and a salad and this makes a very nourishing meal. If available, several leaves of fresh basil, chopped fine, will give added flavor. Sometimes I also add 1/2 cup grated or cubed potatoes. The longer minestrone is cooked, the better will be the flavor. Our Cabernet goes well with this recipe.

Sylvia Sebastiani
Sebastiani Vineyards

Sylvia Sebastiani is also the author of "Mangianio," the classic Italian cookbook.

Corn Chowder

3 cups corn kernels
1/4 cup onion, chopped
4 cups milk
1/2 cup water

4 tablespoons margarine
3 tablespoons flour
1 1/2 teaspoon salt
4 tablespoons jalapeno mustard

In a saucepan, combine corn, onion, water and salt. Bring to a boil then simmer, covered for 15 minutes, stirring occasionally. Meanwhile, melt butter and add flour, milk and mustard. Cook and stir until thick and bubbly. Gradually add to corn mixture. Simmer over low heat for 3 minutes, stirring constantly. Crumbled bacon is a delicious garnish. Serves 6.

Serve with Martinelli Sauvignon Blanc.

Julie Martinelli
Martinelli Vineyards

Dried Tomato, Spinach and Wild Rice Soup

2 teaspoons olive oil
1 pound onions, coarsely chopped
2 large cloves garlic, minced
1/2 cup wild rice

6 cups chicken broth
1/2 cup Sonoma dried tomato bits
1 teaspoon pepper
1/2 pound fresh spinach leaves,
    trimmed and washed

Heat oil in Dutch oven over medium heat; add onions and garlic. Saute, stirring, 3 minutes. Stir in rice; saute, stirring 1 minute. Add broth; bring to boil, cover and simmer 40 to 50 minutes until rice is tender. Add tomato bits and pepper. Simmer 5 minutes longer. Stir in spinach; heat just until wilted. Serves 4 to 6.

Timbercrest Farms

Chilled Cranberry Soup

1 package cranberries
1 quart of apple juice
1/4 to 1/2 cup sugar (to taste)

chestnuts (optional)
cream (optional)

Heat apple juice to a boil. Add cranberries, return to boil. Reduce heat, boil gently for 10 minutes, stirring occasionally. Blend sugar, strain and chill. You can garnish with a dollop of cream and minced chestnuts. Serves 20.

Serve with Lyeth Alexander Valley white wine.

Donna Wegener, Chef de Cuisine
Lyeth Vineyards

Cream of Avocado Soup

4 large ripe avocados
3 cups chicken broth
1/2 teaspoon salt

pinch white pepper
1/2 teaspoon Worcestershire
1 cup light cream

Peel, pit and cube avocados, then puree in blender. In a saucepan mix avocado puree, chicken broth, salt, pepper, and Worcestershire. Heat to boiling point, stirring occasionally. Stir in 1 cup light cream. Cover and simmer 10 minutes. Serve soup hot; garnish each bowl with croutons or popcorn. Serve 6.

This is one from my own file and I use it frequently when avocadoes are in season. Try to get the large Haas type, if possible. VMH.

SALADS

Spinach, Bacon and Lily Salad

1 pound young spinach
6 slices lean bacon
3-4 tiger lily blossoms
your favorite vinaigrette

Cook some young spinach leaves for 1 minute, drain and dry. Arrange the crunchy spinach in a shallow earthenware bowl. Fry bacon until very crisp. Drain on paper towels and crumble over spinach. Toss the salad in a little sharp vinaigrette and finally add the torn petals of tiger lilies. Serves 4.

Serve with Bandiera White Zinfandel.

Bandiera Winery

Over the centuries, flowers and herbs have been used to enhance the aesthetics and flavor of cuisines around the world. This salad and the salmon recipe, also from Bandiera, are wonderful examples of "Cooking with Flowers."

Spinach & Cottage Cheese Salad
with Raspberry & Mustard Vinegarette

1/3 cup red raspberry vinegar
1/3 cup pure olive oil or
  California avacado oil
1 tablespoon soy sauce
2 large cloves fresh garlic, pressed
1 bunch fresh spinach, washed and
  drained, stems removed

fresh ground pepper to taste
1/4 cup sweet-n-hot mustard
1 pint small curd cottage cheese,
  rinsed and drained
1 basket ripe cherry tomatoes,
  washed and stems removed
salt

Mix together red raspberry vinegar, oil, mustard, soy sauce, garlic, salt and pepper until well blended. Place spinach in large salad bowl and arrange cherry tomatoes around the edge of the bowl. Sprinkle cottage cheese in center. Pour desired amount of dressing over salad. Toss until blended. Serve immediately. Makes 4 to 6 servings.

Carmen Kozlowski
Kozlowski Farms

Turkey Fruit Salad

4 cups chopped cooked turkey
1 cup chopped apple
1 cup chopped walnuts
1 cup seedless grapes

1 cup pineapple tidbits
1/2 cup mayonnaise
1 teaspoon curry powder
1 tablespoon lemon juice

Cut turkey and apple into 1 inch pieces. Place turkey and all fruit into a large bowl. In a small bowl mix the curry powder, mayonnaise and lemon juice, thoroughly. Add to the turkey and fruit and refrigerate for at least one hour before serving. Serves 6 to 8 persons. Maraschino cherries can be added for color.

A crispy delicious salad that can be prepared ahead and is excellent for entertaining. VMH

Endive with Golden Caviar

8 ounces of fresh golden caviar*
2-5 whole endives
2 shallots
1 spring onion

8 ounce package cream cheese
  (room temperature)
1/2 cup sour cream or yogurt
2 tablespoon lemon juice
chives for garnish

Mince shallots and spring onion in food processor. Add cream cheese and lemon juice. Blend well. Add sour cream or yogurt to processor. Pulse a few times, just enough to mix through. Shortly before serving, trim ends from endive and drain leaves, cup-side down, on paper towels for a few minutes. Lay out leaves, cut-side up. Put 1 tablespoon of cream mixture in stem end of each leaf. Arrange three leaves on small, chilled plates as a first course and sprinkle with chives. Serves 8.

*You may get fresh caviar from a good fishmonger or deli. Do not settle for the article sold in jars which is too salty and metallic in flavor.

This course is nicely complemented by our Sauvignon Blanc.

Barbara Winiarski, Co-Owner
Stag's Leap Wine Cellars

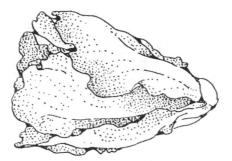

Fennel and Parsley Salad with Smoked Salmon and Grana Cheese

1 medium fennel bulb (reserve
  4 sprigs of fronds for garnish)
1/2 bunch Italian parsley leaves
  (very coarsely chopped)
1/2 cup extra virgin olive oil
3 teaspoons olive oil

1 teaspoon lemon juice
1/3 cup Balsamic vinegar
1 ounce Grana cheese
  shavings
4 ounces smoked salmon strips
salt and pepper to taste

Trim, then halve the fennel bulb, cut out the core then slice it paper thin (preferably on meat slicer). Toss fennel slices and parsley with olive oils, vinegar, lemon juice, and season to taste and divide onto 4 plates. Place smoked salmon strips on top and garnish with fennel fronds. Serves 4.

This delightfully refreshing salad is perfect with Chandon Reserve.

By Chef Philippe Jeanty, Chef de Cuisine
Domaine Chandon

Orzo and Spinach Salad

3/4 pound orzo (Greek rice-shaped pasta)
2 tablespoons olive oil
1/2 cup olive oil
3 tablespoons wine vinegar
3 tablespoons lemon juice
1 teaspoon salt
1/2 teaspoon freshly ground pepper
1 teaspoon Dijon mustard
1 small clove garlic, minced
pinch thyme
3 tablespoons feta cheese, crumbled

1/2 teaspoon dried oregano
1/4 teaspoon ground cumin
1 bunch spinach, washed, in bite-sized pieces
3 tablespoons toasted pine nuts
1/2 cup pitted Kalamata olives, slivered*
1 sweet red pepper, chopped
1/4 cup minced scallion (green & white)
2 teaspoons capers, rinsed & drained

Cook the orzo according to package directions to al dente, drain, run under cold water to stop cooking, then drain thoroughly. Toss with 2 tablespoons olive oil. Prepare the dressing by combining the remaining olive oil with lemon juice, vinegar, herbs and spices, whisking until smooth.

Place the orzo in a large bowl and toss with the dressing. Add spinach, olives, red pepper, scallions and capers and toss to combine. (Can be held, refrigerated, at this point for several hours.) At serving time, add crumbled feta cheese and garnish with toasted pine nuts. Serves 6-8.

*Ripe black olives may be substituted for Kalamata, if necessary. The addition of 3/4 pound tiny cooked shrimp makes this into a very nice entre salad.

Mary Evely, Chef
Simi Winery

Asparagus and Red Pepper Salad

1 small red pepper, roasted
zest of 1 orange, finely grated
1 pound fresh asparagus, ends
  trimmed and stalks peeled
1 1/2 tablespoons sugar

1 tablespoon soy sauce
1 tablespoon sesame oil
5 tablespoons peanut oil
1 tablespoon Chinese rice vinegar
1 tablespoon sesame seeds,
  toasted

Cut the roasted pepper lengthwise into 1/8 inch strips. In a pan large enough to hold asparagus spears lying flat, cook asparagus approximately 4 minutes until crisp and tender. Drain well and pat dry. In a small bowl, whisk together orange zest, sugar, soy sauce, sesame oil, peanut oil and Chinese rice vinegar. (Dressing can be prepared ahead of time.) Arrange asparagus spears on serving plate with tips pointed out in a circular fashion. Lay red pepper in strips over asparagus. Drizzle dressing over plate and refrigerate for at least 4 hours. Serve at room temperature. Sprinkle toasted sesame seeds on top. Serves 4.

Our Sonoma County Fume Blanc is suggested to enhance this salad.

Rhonda Carano, Co-Owner
Ferrari-Carano Vineyards & Winery

Chicken Curry Salad

2 chicken breasts, skinned, boned
1/2 teaspoon onion, diced
1/2 teaspoon thyme
1 can of water chestnuts, drained
  and coarsely chopped
1/2 can sliced palm hearts drained
3/4 cups of sugar roasted peanuts
  and cashews, coarsely chopped

1/2 cup mayonnaise
1/4 cup orange juice
1 teaspoon curry powder
1 small box of fried onion rings
1 cup fried chow mein noodles
1/2 cup water
1/2 cup white wine
1/2 teaspoon salt

Bring water, wine, thyme, onion, and salt to a boil. Add chicken breast, cover pan and simmer very slowly for 30 minutes. Lift off heat and let cool in the broth. (To microwave: bring broth to a boil, add chicken breast and cover - cook 10-12 minutes on medium-low and let cool in broth.) Cut chicken breasts into bite sized pieces. In a large bowl, mix in mayonnaise, orange juice and curry thoroughly. Add all other ingredients (including chicken) except onion rings and noodles, and mix until everything is coated with the mayonnaise. Just before serving mix in onion rings and noodles. Serves 6.

Serve with Louis Martini Chardonnay.

Louis M. Martini Winery

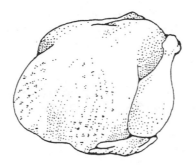

Wild Rice Salad

6 cups cooked wild rice, preferably cooked in chicken stock
6 scallions, cut in thin diagonal slices
1/2 cup skinless almonds, roasted and roughly chopped
salt & pepper to taste

1 head radicchio, coarsely chopped
2 ears corn, blanched 2 minutes, slice kernels off cob
2-3 tablespoons fresh dill, chopped

Combine all ingredients. Pour vinaigrette over rice salad (see below). Check for seasonings.

VINAIGRETTE:

2 teaspoons Dijon mustard
2 teaspoons Balsamic vinegar
1/2 cup hazelnut oil

1/2 cup corn oil
salt & pepper

Blend all ingredients.

NOTES FROM THE CHEF:

The beauty of this salad is its versatility with many wines. With its hazelnut oil vinaigrette, it will go nicely with a Chateau Souverain Chardonnay. Because of the dill, it will also show well with a Chateau Souverain Sauvignon Blanc. Grilled chicken, shrimp, white meat dishes are fine accompaniments for this. To serve the salad with a red meat such as lamb or beef in order to pair it with a Chateau Souverain Cabernet Sauvignon, merely use walnut oil instead of hazelnut and replace the almonds with toasted walnuts or pecans. Finally, change the herb to tarragon.

Patricia Windisch,
Executive Chef/General Manager
Chateau Souverain Restaurant

Classic Berry Vinaigrette

1/2 cup blueberry, red or
  black raspberry vinegar

salt & pepper to taste
1/2 cup light olive oil

Blend all ingredients together in a small bowl with wire whisk.

WITH MUSTARD:

Add 2 large cloves crushed garlic and 2 tablespoons Sweet-n-Hot Mustard to the above recipe.

Use on any tossed salad, coleslaw, bean, pasta or green salad. Serve over sliced tomatoes or cucumbers. Great over chilled cooked carrots, artichokes, beets or broccoli.

Kozlowski Farms

Originally a Kozlowski farm only, Kozlowski Farms now prepares, under their own label, many different products, all from their own farms. Vinegars, jams, jellies, chutneys, mustards, now in gourmet sections to department stores and gourmet shops throughout the country. We seem to find something new every time we go there! RPH

Chardonnay Salad Dressing

8 ounces Sonoma Valley
  Chardonnay
4 peeled shallots
1 clove garlic

3 tablespoons Dijon mustard
3 cups olive oil
2 tablespoons fresh dill

In a non-reactive pan, cook chardonnay until reduced by half. Cool. In a food processor, puree shallots and garlic, add mustard. Add olive oil slowly and steadily. Add dill and wine.

Stephen Bennett-Welch,
The Grist Mill Inn

As served at the Sonoma Valley Vintners' Picnic in the Park.

PASTA
&
GRAINS

Sylvia Sebastiani's Spaghetti Sauce

1 pound ground beef (optional)
4 tablespoons olive oil
4 tablespoons butter
4 stalks celery, chopped
4 onions, chopped
4 cloves garlic, chopped fine
1/4 teaspoon rosemary
1/2 cup dried Italian mushrooms, soaked in 1 cup hot water then chopped

1 large can solid pack tomatoes mashed with liquid
6 8-ounce cans tomato sauce
1 1/2 cups water
1 cup Chablis
1 teaspoon sugar
1/4 teaspoon thyme
1/2 cup parsley, chopped fine
salt & pepper to taste

If using meat, brown meat in olive oil and butter. Add celery and onions until brown, then add garlic. Salt and pepper to taste; then add spices, mushrooms with their liquid, tomatoes and tomato sauce. Rinse tomato sauce cans with water and add to sauce along with wine and sugar. Cook for 3 hours over low heat, stirring occasionally. If not using meat, start by browning onions and celery and proceed as above. Instead of ground meat, a piece of pot roast can be used.

Brown on all sides, proceed as above, letting meat simmer in sauce. After 2 hours, remove meat from sauce and keep warm. Slice and serve as meat course for your dinner. If your family likes their sauce hot, add a small chili pepper, chopped very fine, while sauce is simmering.

This recipe yields a quantity of sauce greater than you would normally use at one time. Freeze the remainder in pint jars, filling 3/4 full. I always keep a supply of frozen sauce on hand - it helps put together numerous meals in a short time.

PASTA COOKING HINT: When boiling pasta, add one teaspoon salt for every 4 cups of water. Also, add one tablespoon of oil so pasta will not stick together while cooking.

Suggested wine: Sebastiani Barbera

Sylvia Sebastiani
Sebastiani Vineyards

Martini Family Pasta Sauce

1 large onion
4 cloves garlic
1 bunch parsley
olive oil
1 large can tomatoes
2 8-ounce cans tomato sauce
1 cup dried porcini mushrooms

1 1/4 teaspoon ground sage
1 1/4 teaspoon ground marjoram
3/4 teaspoon ground thyme
1/2 teaspoon ground nutmeg
1/2 teaspoon ground cloves
salt and pepper to taste
2 bay leaves

Chop onion, garlic, and parsley leaves together. Saute until cooked but not brown in 1/4" olive oil. Add tomatoes, breaking them up, and tomato sauce. Add herbs and spices. In a separate pan, put dried mushrooms and cover with water. Bring to a boil and simmer slowly until tender. Pour liquid into a glass to settle out any sand. Chop the mushrooms and add to sauce. Decant liquid into sauce. Cook very slowly until an avenue can be formed when stirred, about 3 hours.

Serve with Martini Barbera.

This is a wonderful old family recipe from the Louis M. Martini Winery.

Spaghetti Sauce

1 large onion
2 large cloves garlic
1 small bunch parsley
2 stalks celery with leaves
2 14-1/2 ounce cans chopped
  tomatoes (not stewed)
2 mild Italian sausages
olive oil

2-3 cans tomato paste
2 cups chicken bouillon cubes
2 cups water
1/2 teaspoon brown sugar
salt and pepper to taste
1/2 cup Cocktail Sherry
2 hot Italian sausages

Chop all vegetables in chopper. Mince garlic and saute in 2 tablespoons olive oil for 10 minutes on low. Add tomatoes, tomato paste, bouillon, water and brown sugar. Meanwhile, fry sausages and drain well. Add sausages and Cocktail Sherry to sauce and simmer 2 to 4 hours.

Jeani Martini
Martini & Prati Wines

Lucy's Tomato Tuna Sauce & Pasta

3/4 to 1 pound tuna filet, 1 inch thick
1/4 cup olive oil
2 tablespoons minced onion
1 tablespoon minced garlic
1/2 cup Chardonnay or Pinot Noir
1 tablespoon cream (optional)

1 can 14 1/2 ounce cut-up tomatoes with juice
1 tablespoon drained, rinsed capers
2 tablespoons pine nuts
1 tablespoons parsley

Heat olive oil in medium saute pan. Add onion and garlic and saute for one minute. Add tuna and wine. Cook about three minutes on each side or until tuna is medium done and will flake into small chunks. Add tomatoes and juice, capers and pine nuts. Simmer until liquid thickens slightly. In the meantime, boil the pasta. While the pasta is cooking, add parsley and cream (if desired) to the sauce. Salt and pepper to taste. Pour over drained pasta and serve hot. Serves six as a first course, four as a main course.

A note from the chef: A recipe that satisfies red or white wine lovers! This is a versatile dish that pairs equally well with a substantial Chardonnay like Rodney Strong Chalk Hill Chardonnay or a soft red like the Rodney Strong River East Pinot Noir. Whichever wine you prefer to drink with dinner, use that also in preparing this recipe.

Lucy Cafaro
Rodney Strong Vineyards

Manicotti

1 cup chard or spinach, cooked
well drained and chopped
1 cup cottage cheese
1/2 cup Parmesan cheese, grated
1 egg
1 garlic bud, sliced

1 tablespoon basil or parsley,
chopped
1/2 teaspoon salt
1/4 teaspoon pepper
1 package manicotti

Mix well, stuff uncooked manicotti and place in buttered baking dish in single layer, leaving space to allow for expansion during baking. Cover with the following sauce.

SAUCE:

1 pound ground chuck, browned
1/2 pound pork sausage, browned
1 medium onion, chopped
1 teaspoon salt
1/8 teaspoon pepper
1 4-ounce can slice mushrooms,
undrained

1 teaspoon Italian herbs
1/2 cup Zinfandel
1 30-ounce can solid pack
tomatoes
1 6-ounce can tomato
paste

To browned meat mixture add onion, seasonings and Zinfandel. Simmer until flavors are well blended. Cover manicotti with sauce, sprinkle with Parmesan cheese. Cover with foil and bake for 1 to 1 1/4 hours in oven at 375°.

Serve with Sausel Zinfandel or Cabernet Sauvignon.

Cindy Martin & Roselee Demostene, Co-Owners
Sausal Winery

Rotelle Pasta with
Smoked Turkey, Broccoli and Peppers

6 cups small broccoli florets
1 pound rotelle pasta (fusilli
  may be substituted)
6 tablespoons unsalted butter
6 tablespoons olive oil
4 garlic cloves, minced
1 cup roasted red peppers, diced

1 1/2 pound smoked turkey, skin
  removed and diced
  (must be smoked)
1 1/2 cups chicken broth
freshly grated Romano cheese
3/4 teaspoon dried red pepper
  flakes

Cook broccoli in boiling water just until crisp tender, about 2 minutes. Using slotted spoon, transfer broccoli to bowl of ice water to cool; reserve water in pot. Drain broccoli and pat dry. Return water to boil. Add pasta and cook until al dente. Drain thoroughly. Melt butter with olive oil over low heat. Add garlic and red pepper flakes and saute until garlic is tender. Add turkey and saute until heated through, about 3 to 4 minutes. Mix broccoli, pasta, roasted peppers and stock into turkey mixture. Increase heat to high and cook until broccoli has absorbed most of the liquid, stirring often. Shave Romano cheese over the top. Serves 6-8.

* If jar-packed peppers are used, be sure to drain.

Serve with Pine Ridge Chardonnay, Knollside Cuvee.

Nancy F. Andrus, Co-Owner
Pine Ridge Winery

Pasta with Shrimp,
Asparagus and Cream Sauce

1 pound pasta
4 tablespoons butter
4 tablespoons olive oil
3 cloves garlic, crushed
1 pound asparagus
1 pound medium shrimp

1 cup Sauvignon Blanc
1-1/2 cups whipping cream
3 tablespoons arrowroot
salt and white pepper
cilantro

Boil water with 2 tablespoons olive oil and salt. Cook pasta. Wash and drain shrimp; saute in 2 tablespoons butter. Add asparagus and steam about 2 minutes, set aside. Heat butter and remaining oil and saute garlic. Add wine and when it has evaporated, add cream and arrowroot and whisk until thickened, correct salt and pepper. In large bowl, toss drained pasta, shrimp and asparagus with sauce and sprinkle with chopped cilantro. Preparation time: 40 minutes. Serves 6.

Serve with Chalk Hill Sauvignon Blanc.

Chalk Hill Winery

Tomato/Basil Pasta

1 pound fresh pasta (preferably
  corkscrew)
6 whole tomatoes, chopped
1 cup fresh basil, chopped
2 whole garlic cloves

1/2 pound of Brie (rind
  removed) cut in 1" squares
1/4 cup cream
salt & pepper to taste

Boil pasta according to directions on package. If using fresh pasta, boil only 5 to 6 minutes. Return to warm pan. Keep pan on warm burner. Add all the above ingredients. Mix until all Brie has melted. Serve at room temperature. Serves 6.

We suggest serving with Fisher Creek Insignia Chardonnay.

Juelle Fisher, Co-Owner
Fisher Vineyards

Ravioli Fritti Filled With Corn and Basil

1 cup fresh or frozen corn kernels
1 clove garlic, chopped
1 tablespoon fresh basil, chopped
1 tablespoon butter
1/4 cup milk

1/2 teaspoon salt
1/2 cup ricotta cheese
2 tablespoons finely grated
  Parmigiana
fresh ground black pepper

Combine corn, garlic and basil in the bowl of a food processor and process until corn is chopped quite small but do not puree. Combine with milk, butter and salt in a small heavy saucepan. Bring to boil, lower heat and simmer 3-4 minutes or longer until very thick. Add the ricotta and stir over high heat for another minute or so to evaporate some of the moisture. Add Parmigiana and a little fresh ground pepper. Taste and add salt as necessary. Chill the mixture well before filling the ravioli.

PASTA DOUGH:*

2 large eggs
1 1/4 cup all-purpose flour
1 teaspoon salt

Combine all ingredients in a food processor and process until the dough just begins to hold together. Transfer to a lightly floured board and knead by hand until the dough is soft and supple, incorporating more flour if necessary. Pasta dough for ravioli should be quite softer than that for noodles, but not wet or sticky. Let dough rest, covered for at least 1/2 hour before rolling.

Roll out dough in your pasta machine to the next to last setting. Place rounded spoonfulls of filling on the lower half of the dough, fold dough over, press dough down around filling. Ravioli should be about 1 1/2 inches square. Cut ravioli with fluted wheel (or sharp knife if you don't have one) leaving very little border around the filling. Press edges together well or the ravioli will break open while cooking. If your dough is nice and moist and not floured excessively it should stick together with no problem. If not, you may need to moisten the edges with a little water before pressing together.

Place the ravioli on a floured baking sheet and turn occasionally to prevent sticking. Once they are dry enough to not stick, cover them with a towel. They can be made an hour or two in advance of cooking.

Cooking: Add your favored cooking oil to a skillet to a depth of at least 1 1/2 inches. Heat to 350°. Add as many ravioli as the pan will hold without crowding and fry until nicely browned on each side. Transfer to absorbent paper. Keep in a warm oven while frying subsequent batches. Serve on a tray or platter. Don't mound the ravioli or the moist filling may make ravioli soggy. Yield: about 32 ravioli.

*Notes: If you're not experienced at making your own pasta dough, or would rather not bother, you can purchase sheets of dough from markets or delicatessens that sell fresh pasta noodles. It is really important that fried ravioli be well-filled. Boiled ravioli are served in a sauce so that the pasta is flavored both inside and out, fried ravioli are only flavored on the inside.

Suggested wine: Sterling Vineyards 1989 Estate Chardonnay

Richard Alexi, Wine & Food Consultant
Sterling Vineyards

Fettucine al Pesto

1 cup parsley	1 teaspoon or so of salt
1/2 cup olive oil	1/2 teaspoon fresh ground pepper
1/2 cup cream	1 cup grated Parmesan cheese
1/3 cup butter, softened	1 cup chopped fresh basil leaves,
4 cloves garlic, cropped fine	firmly packed
1/2 cup chopped pine nuts	2 tablespoon boiling water
2 pounds fettucine	8 quarts boiling salted water

Place parsley, olive oil, cream, butter, garlic, salt, pepper, cheese, basil and pine nuts in a sauce pan and stir. Reduce heat to low; add 2 tablespoons of water and cover. Simmer over medium heat for 10 minutes, stirring frequently. Meanwhile, cook fettucine in 8 quarts of salted water according to directions on pasta package. Drain and toss the sauce and fettucine together lightly. Serve immediately. Makes 8 servings.

Magliulo's Restaurant & Pensione

Sonoma Farmer's Market Lasagna

2 cups Swiss chard, baby bok choy and spring greens, blanched, drained and chopped
1 cup zucchini, blanched and sliced press out excess water
2 cups fresh jack cheese curd mixed with 1/2 cup cream (or 2 1/2 cups ricotta)
4 eggs plus 2 egg yolks
1/2 teaspoon salt
1 cup dry Jack cheese, grated

1/2 teaspoon white pepper
2 cups Sonoma Valley sparkling wine
2 cups heavy cream, heated
1 shallot, minced
1 teaspoon flour
1 teaspoon clarified butter
fresh lasagna noodles, enough for three layers
1 cut part skim Jack cheese, grated

In a food processor, blend cheese curd/cream mixture, 4 eggs, salt and pepper. In a saucepan, combine shallots and wine and cook until liquid is reduced by 1/2. Add heated cream to wine. Mix flour and butter to make roux to add to liquid to thicken as necessary. Reserve 1 cup of cream sauce for lasagna topping. Cook fresh lasagna in large pot of boiling water and drain.

Assemble in a 9x12x4 inch pan. Cover pan bottom with thin layer of cream sauce; add layer of pasta; add 1/2 cheese mixture, spreading evenly; add layer of chopped greens; add layer of sliced zucchini; sprinkle with the grated Jack cheese, drizzle with cream sauce. Repeat and top with layer of pasta. Pour reserved cup of cream sauce over top layer of pasta and sprinkle with dry Jack cheese. Bake in preheated oven at 350° for 40 minutes.

Serve with a Sonoma Valley Chardonnay.

Keith Filipello (Wild Thyme), Early LeClaire (Sonoma Chefs)

Courtesy of Sonoma Valley Cuisine Society.

Cous-Cous (Near East Pasta)

1/2 cup cous-cous
3/4 cup water
2 tablespoons olive oil
1/2 cup snow peas
1/2 cup sliced carrots

1/2 cup chopped red pepper
1 teaspoon chopped fresh mint
1 tablespoon chopped parsley
1 tablespoon lemon juice
salt & pepper to taste

Cook cous-cous according to directions on box using olive oil instead of butter. Remove ends and strings from snow peas and cook in boiling water to "al dente," about 3 minutes. Drain and rinse in cold water. Clean and slice carrot and cook to "al dente," about 5 minutes in boiling water. Drain and run cold water over. Combine all ingredients. Let stand in refrigerator approximately 1 hour or until well chilled. If dry, add more French dressing, olive oil to lemon juice 2 to 1. Serves 6.

Serve with Louis Martini Chardonnay.

Louis M. Martini Winery

Saffron Rice

1 shallot, minced
1 clove garlic, minced
1 tablespoon butter
1/4 teaspoon saffron threads

1 1/2 cup chicken stock
1 cup white rice
1 teaspoon thyme, dried
salt and white pepper

Saute shallots, garlic in butter briefly. Add remaining ingredients and bring to a boil. Cover and bake for 35-45 minutes until all the liquid is gone. Fluff with a fork and serve. Makes 2-3 cups.

Napa Beaucanon Winery

Paella with Dried Tomatoes

1 1/2 tablespoons olive oil
6 chicken legs (about 1 1/2 pounds), skinned
1 1/4 cups chopped onion
1 cup Julienned green bell pepper
2 to 3 cloves garlic, minced
1 1/2 cups long-grain converted rice
3 cups chicken broth or bouillon
1 can (14 1/2 ounce) whole peeled tomatoes, with juice
1 tablespoon chopped fresh oregano or 1 teaspoon dried oregano leaves
1 tablespoon chopped fresh thyme or 1 teaspoon dried thyme
1/4 to 1/2 teaspoon red pepper flakes
1 1/2 pounds scrubbed clams, and/or mussels debearded
3/4 pound medium shrimp, peeled
1 cup frozen peas, thawed
1 1/2 cups Sonoma dried tomato halves
1 cup dry white wine
salt & pepper to taste

Heat oil in Dutch oven over medium heat; add chicken and saute until brown on all sides, about 10 minutes. Add onion, bell pepper and garlic; saute, stirring, 3 minutes. Add rice, broth, canned tomatoes, dried tomatoes, wine, oregano, thyme and pepper flakes. Bring to a boil, cover and simmer about 20 minutes until liquid is almost absorbed. Stir in clams and/or mussels; cook about 6 minutes until shells begin to open. Stir in shrimp and peas; cook 2 to 3 minutes until shrimp are opaque and all clam and/or mussel shells open. Season with salt and pepper. 6 servings.

Waltenspiel's Kitchen
Timbercrest Farms

Fettucine with Scallops and Peas in Saffron Butter Sauce

2 cups shelled fresh peas, or
  a 10 ounce package of frozen
  peas
1 pound fresh fettucine
court bouillon

1/2 stick unsalted butter, cut into
  bits and softened
1 1/4 pounds sea scallops
1 cup saffron butter sauce
Parmesan cheese

In a saucepan of boiling salted water cook the fresh peas until tender, drain well. Cook the pasta in a large pot of boiling water until al dente. Drain and transfer to a large skillet with melted butter in it. Add the peas and salt and pepper to taste and heat the mixture through. Cook your scallops (rinsed, patted dry and any large scallops halved) in a court bouillon broth, drain and add the scallops to the pasta mixture. Add butter saffron sauce and toss with Parmesan cheese. Divide on plates and serve. Serves 6.

SAFFRON BUTTER SAUCE:

1/4 teaspoon crumbled saffron
  threads
2 tablespoons minced shallots
2 tablespoons white wine vinegar

3 tablespoons dry white wine
3 tablespoons heavy cream
2 sticks cold unsalted butter,
  cut into pieces

In a small heavy saucepan combine the saffron, shallots, vinegar and wine, bring to a simmer over moderate heat. Reduce to about 2 tablespoons. Add the cream and simmer, whisking occasionally until reduced to about 2 tablespoons (sauce can be prepared up to this point 1 hour in advance and kept covered at room temperature; bring to a simmer before continuing). Season the mixture with salt and pepper, reduce heat and whisk in butter a piece at a time, lifting pan from the heat occasionally to cool the mixture and adding each new piece of butter before the previous one has completely melted. (The sauce should not be to hot to liquefy.) Remove from heat and correct seasoning. Makes about 1 cup.

We serve our Alexander Valley Chardonnay with this entree.

Rhonda Carano, Co-Owner
Ferrari-Carano Vineyards & Winery

Risotto with Three Grains

1/4 pound butter
4 onions, chopped fine
1 carrot, chopped fine
1 1/2 teaspoon quatre-espices*
3 cups Zinfandel
1 quart chicken stock
bouquet garni

1 cup converted rice
1 cup wild rice
1 cup coarse cracked wheat
1/2 pound fresh mushrooms
 (boleti or chanterelles)
salt and pepper
2 cloves garlic, minced
chopped parsley

Heat 2 tablespoons butter, add onions and carrots and saute until onions are golden. Add quatre-espices, wine and broth. Bring to a boil; add bouquet garni and reduce to 6 cups. Remove the bouquet garni but do not strain. Heat 4 tablespoons butter in heavy bottomed pot (cast iron). Add rice; stir until well-coated and lightly browned. Add 2 cup of stock reduction. Cover with paper towel and lid, and cook until done. Heat 4 tablespoons of butter in another pot.

Add wild rice and toss quickly to coat and heat. Add 3 cups of stock reduction, cover and cook until liquid has been absorbed and grains have opened, about 30 minutes. Heat 4 tablespoons of butter in another pot. Add cracked wheat and toss to coat. Add the last cup of stock reduction. Remove from heat and keep covered until all liquid has been absorbed. Heat last 2 tablespoons of butter in sauce pan. Add sliced mushrooms, salt and pepper, and saute until all juices run out of mushrooms. Add juices to the cracked wheat. Continue sauteing the mushrooms until golden. Mix mushrooms with all grains. Adjust seasoning. Add garlic and parsley. Serves 8-12.

*Quatre-espices: 3/4 teaspoon cinnamon; 2 teaspoon allspice; 1/2 teaspoon ground gloves; 1/2 teaspoon ground cardamon; 3/4 teaspoon grated nutmeg; 2 teaspoon coriander.

Serve with 1989 De Loach Vineyards Estate Bottled Zinfandel.

Christine DeLoach
DeLoach Vineyards

MEATS

Spirited Ragout

1 pound beef stew meat
1 pound lamb stew meat
1 pound pork stew meat
2 cups Petite Sirah or Merlot
3 tablespoons chopped fresh sage
2 teaspoons ground cumin
sprinkle of freshly ground pepper
4 tablespoons butter
3 cloves garlic, minced

1 teaspoon salt
1 cup beef stock
1 sweet potato, steamed or
   blanched
2 turnips, steamed or blanched
1 small bunch broccoli, steamed
   or blanched
3 carrots, steamed or blanched
2 ounces bittersweet chocolate,
   chopped

Marinate the meats in the wine, sage, cumin, and pepper overnight. Lift meat out of marinade and dry with paper towels. Bring the marinade to a boil and strain. Throw out any solids. Melt butter in a large skillet and add the meat. Cook until browned. Add the garlic and cook 1 minute more. Add the marinade, stock and salt. Simmer about 1 hour or until meat seem tender but not falling apart. Add the chocolate and let melt completely. Add the cooked vegetables and simmer about 15 minutes. Correct seasonings with salt and pepper. Serve over cooked rice (seasoned with a little cumin and butter). Serves 8.

Serve with Martini Merlot or Reserve Petite Sirah.

Louis Martini Winery

This recipe may well become a family favorite of yours. The combinations of meats, the intermingling of the spices with the wine and the chocolate!!!

Sima
(Stuffed Breast of Veal)

1 breast or shoulder of veal with
  a pocket cut in
1 onion
4 tablespoons oil
2 tablespoons butter
2 cloves garlic, pressed
2 packages frozen chopped
  spinach or 2 bunches fresh
  spinach, well cooked, drained and
  chopped fine

1/2 cup chopped parsley
5 eggs
2 cups bread crumbs
3/4 cup grated Parmesan cheese
dash of basil
salt & pepper to taste
1 teaspoon rosemary
1 cup Pinot Noir Blanc
  or Chardonnay
1/3 cup butter

Saute onion in oil and butter, adding 1 clove garlic last. Add spinach, parsley, eggs, bread crumbs, cheese, and seasonings, mixing well with a fork. Stuff into pocket of veal and sew with a coarse needle and thread, closing completely. Place in roasting pan and rub with 1 clove garlic. Sprinkle with rosemary and baste with wine and butter. Roast uncovered at 350° until brown, about 1 hour, basting occasionally. Serves 6-8.

Suggested wine: Sebastiani Chardonnay

By Sylvia Sebastiani
Sebastiani Winery

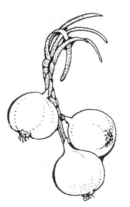

Osso Buco

3 pounds veal shanks, cut into 6
   pieces about 2 inches thick
1/2 cup flour
1/4 cup butter
1 tablespoon olive oil
2 teaspoons salt
1/2 teaspoon freshly ground black
   pepper
1 medium yellow onion, chopped
1/2 cup chopped carrots
1/2 cup chopped celery
1 teaspoon garlic, finely chopped

1/4 teaspoon marjoram
1/4 teaspoon thyme
1 teaspoon lemon rind, grated
1 teaspoon orange rind, grated
2 anchovy filets, mashed
1 cup dry white wine
1 cup tomato pulp
2 cups chicken stock
1/2 cup parsley, finely chopped
1 bay leaf
1/2 cup cognac

Ask your butcher to prepare the veal shanks. Roll the shanks in flour and brown on all sides in 3 tablespoons butter and the olive oil. Salt and pepper to taste. Add the onion, carrots, celery, garlic, marjoram, thyme, lemon and orange rind and the anchovy if desired, and cook over very low heat for approximately 10 minutes, or until the vegetables are soft.

Add the wine and cook until almost completely evaporated. Add tomato pulp and chicken stock, cover and cook over low heat until tender, about 1 1/2 hours. If sauce is evaporating too quickly add a little chicken broth. Add bay leaf and simmer.

When ready to serve, finish with the remaining butter and cognac and sprinkle with chopped parsley. Serves 6.

We serve our Alexander Valley Cabernet Sauvignon with this.

Rhonda Carano, Co-Owner
Ferrari-Carano Vineyards & Winery

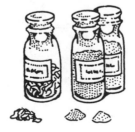

Zin Venison

venison steaks   Melted butter
soy sauce   Zinfandel

Cut venison steaks, about 1/2 inch thick in pieces about 3 inches square. Arrange in glass dish and cover with a mixture of one part soy sauce to two parts Zinfandel. Cover dish tightly and let marinate at least overnight, or up to three days. Remove from marinade and with a very sharp knife make cuts about 1/4 inch apart halfway through meat. Turn and score other side in opposite direction.

Dredge in flour and brown in melted butter, cooking only long enough to crisp each side. Serve at once, perhaps with mushrooms cooked quickly in the pan you cooked the venison in, baked potatoes, and a leafy salad.

Helen Caswell suggest her Zinfandel with this entree.

Helen Caswell, Owner
Caswell Winter Creek Farm and Vineyards

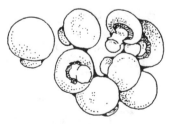

Saltimbocca Ala Romana

1 1/2 pounds veal scaloppine
  (approximately 3x4 inch pieces)
8 slices proscuitto (cut into
  3x3 inch pieces)
12 leaves sage, cut in half
  (dry can be substituted)

flour
3 tablespoons butter
1/2 cup oil
salt and pepper
1/2 cup Chardonnay
toothpicks

Pound the veal. Put a slice of prosciutto and a leaf of sage over the meat. Roll and secure with toothpicks. Dust lightly with flour. Melt the butter and oil in a frying pan. Brown the veal very quickly on both sides over a high heat, heat and cook for 5 minutes maximum. Transfer the meat to a platter and place in low heat oven to keep warm. Pour off oil in pan and add the wine to the pan and deglaze it. Reduce the sauce. Pour the sauce over the meat. Serves 6.

Serve with Geyser Peak Reserve Alexander.

Anne Vercelli
Geyser Peak Winery

83

Porcini Veal Stew

1 ounce porcini mushrooms
1 cup water
1 cup all-purpose flour
1 tablespoon salt
1 teaspoon pepper
1 teaspoon cumin
1 bay leaf
1/4 cup olive oil

3 pounds lean veal stew meat
6 garlic cloves
1 onion, chopped
12 ounces fresh mushrooms
1 can beef broth
1 cup Cabernet Sauvignon
12 boiler onions
1/2 cup chopped parsley

Combine porcini and water in sauce pan and bring to boil; set aside. Combine dry ingredients and dredge meat in mixture; brown meat in olive oil in Dutch oven. Remove meat and add onions, garlic and fresh mushrooms; saute. Add wine, beef broth, browned meat, onions and parsley. Bake in oven for 1 1/2 hours. Preparation time: 2 hours. 6 servings.

Recommended: Chalk Hill Cabernet Sauvignon

Chalk Hill Winery

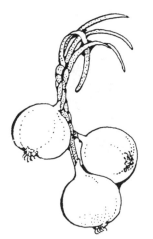

Veal Ring with Curry Sauce

2 eggs
1 1/3 cup coarse cracker crumbs
3/4 cup milk
2 teaspoons salt
1/8 teaspoon pepper

1 1/2 tablespoon steak sauce
1/2 cup onion, minced fine
1/3 cup green pepper, minced
2 1/2 pounds ground veal
3/4 pounds ground pork

Beat eggs, add milk and all other ingredients. Mix until well blended. Pack into greased 8 cup ring mold. Bake at 325° for 1 1/2 hours. Serve on large plate and fill center with Raisin Coconut Pilaf. Pour some sauce over top. Serve rest of sauce in sauce boat.

CURRY SAUCE:

1/2 cup minced onion
3 tablespoons butter
1/4 cup flour
1/4 teaspoon salt

1/4 teaspoon nutmeg
2 teaspoons curry powder
2 cups chicken broth

Saute onions. Add flour and seasonings. Add liquid and simmer slowly 1/2 hour.

RAISIN COCONUT PILAF:

4 cups hot cooked rice
1 cup golden seedless raisins
1/2 cup toasted coconut

1 tablespoon orange rind
1 tablespoon minced parsley
1 tablespoon minced pimento

Mix well and heat.

Serve dry white wine with this.

This recipe is from my own "Entertaining" file. It has been a great success for many years. VMH.

Pork with Apples and Ginger

3 pounds boneless pork loin, cut into 2 inch cubes

2 apples, peeled, cored and chopped

1 tablespoon fresh minced ginger

2-4 apples, peeled and cut in half (put in lemon water to keep from browning)

1 onion, peeled and finely chopped

1 tablespoon butter, margarine or oil

wooden skewers (soaked in water)

Melt butter in saucepan. Saute onions until almost caramelized. Add ginger and chopped apples. Cook about 15 minutes. While fresh applesauce is cooking, prepare pork and remaining apples (the lemon juice will prevent them from turning brown). A wooden skewer will hold 3 pieces of pork separated by 2 pieces of apple. Place in a casserole dish. Pour applesauce over the pork skewers and marinade for a couple of hours or while you are preparing the rest of the meal. Grill or broil pork skewers approximately 10 minutes, making sure not to overcook. While pork cooks, boil the remaining sauce to serve. Serves 4-6. Preparation time 30-45 minutes. Can be prepared ahead of time and left to marinade in refrigerator overnight.

Wine: Sea Ridge Pinot Noir

Dee Wickham
Sea Ridge Winery

Lamb Chops with Vegetables and Fruit

6 lamb chops about 6 ounces each
3 kiwi, peeled and scooped into balls
2 cups seedless red or green grapes
24 asparagus spears, trimmed and
sliced diagonally

2 thin cucumbers, peeled and
scooped into balls
1/3 cup fresh parsley
1/3 cup fresh mint

Preheat oven to 350°. Arrange each chop on a piece of foil, season to taste with salt and pepper. Scatter fruit and vegetables around the chops, dividing equally. Sprinkle herbs over all. Seal the foil packets and set on a baking sheet. Bake for 20 minutes for medium rare. Transfer packets to individual serving dishes. Serves 6.

Serve with our 1988 Napa Valley Chardonnay or 1986 Napa Valley Cabernet Sauvignon.

Mrs. Mitsuko Shrem
Clos Pegase Winery

Butterfly Leg of Lamb

1 butterflied leg of lamb
1/2 bottle Pinot Noir
Grey Poupon
Balsamic vinegar

1 tablespoon Worcestershire
Sauce
1 tablespoon soy sauce
4 cloves garlic, minced

Mix Pinot Noir, Gray Poupon, Balsamic vinegar, Worcestershire Sauce, soy sauce, and garlic in 1 gallon ziploc bag. Place lamb in bag and marinate for 24 hours. Barbecue on a hot grill 7 minutes per inch per side. Remove from grill and slice thinly across the grain (as you would a London broil).

Serve with Bouchaine Pinot Noir to 10-12 guests.

Bouchaine Vineyards

Medallions of Pork with
Champagne Mustard Sauce

1 pound pork tenderloin, cut
  into medallions
1 tablespoon butter
1/4 cup Champagne
1/4 teaspoon rosemary

1 teaspoon Dijon mustard
1 teaspoon honey
2 tablespoons demi-glace
4 tablespoons heavy cream

Sprinkle pork lightly with flour, salt and pepper. In a heavy saute pan, melt butter and sear pork on medium-high heat. Cover pan, turn heat to medium-low and cook until pork is done, approximately 10 minutes. Remove medallions to warm plates. Add Champagne and rosemary to saute pan, turn heat to medium-heat, and reduce to approximately 2 tablespoons. Add mustard, honey and demi-glace. Mix well. Add heavy cream. Bring to a boil and serve over pork medallions. Serves 2-3.

Pork tenderloin is a delicious cut of meat which is readily available from your butcher or supermarket. This dish can be prepared in less than 30 minutes, so it is a real life saver when you want to prepare a nice meal but have little time. Serve with a simple pasta type accompaniment such as cous-cous or spaetzle, or with wild rice.

Serve with Korbel Blanc de Noirs Champagne.

F. Korbel & Bros., Inc.

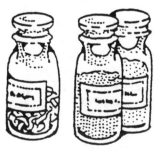

Peaches Stuffed with Pork and Almonds

6 large almost-ripe peaches, unpeeled
1/3 cup slivered almonds
1/3 cup (2 ounces) ground pork
1/4 cup fresh white bread crumbs
1 egg, slightly beaten
1/4 teaspoon almond extract
salt and pepper to taste
2 tablespoons olive oil
salt and pepper to taste

2 tablespoons butter
1/4 cup all-purpose flour
1/4 cup peach brandy
2 cups brown stock or beef consume (brown stock may be purchased frozen in specialty markets)
1/3 cup Brut Champagne
5 whole cloves
fresh mint leaves (optional)

Heat oven to 350°. Slice 1/4 inch from stem end of peaches, so peaches will stand upright. With grapefruit knife or melon baller, cut out peach pit, being careful not to cut through bottom or sides. Toast almonds on baking sheet until golden, 15 minutes. Grind in blender or food processor.

Mix almonds, pork, bread crumbs, egg and almond extract thoroughly; season to taste with salt and pepper. Stuff peaches loosely with mixture. In large skillet, heat oil and butter over medium-low heat. Dip stuffed side of peach into flour; fry peaches, stuffed side down, until golden (7 to 10 minutes). Transfer peaches to flameproof casserole; keep warm. Add brandy to skillet, heat to boiling, scraping bottom with wooden spoon. Add stock, Champagne and cloves; return to boil. Pour over peaches. Bake until pork is done, 45 minutes. Cover loosely, if necessary, to prevent drying.

Transfer peaches to serving platter, stuffing side up; keep warm. Reduce cooking liquid to 3/4 cup over high heat; taste and adjust seasoning with salt and pepper. Pour reduced liquid over peaches; garnish with mint. Serves 6.

Recommended wine: Gloria Ferrer 1985 Carneros Cuvée

Gloria Ferrer Champagne Caves

Mustard-Seed Plush Pork Patties

1/2 cup fine soft fresh bread crumbs from non-sour French bread or farm-style white bread
3 1/2 tablespoons half & half
1 pound ground lean boneless pork (trimmed shoulder, butt, loin ends or chops)
3/4 teaspoon salt

1/8 teaspoon sugar
1 1/2 teaspoons crumbed dry thyme
4 tablespoons unsalted butter
Boston lettuce, tender leaves broken into large pieces
2 teaspoons fresh lemon juice
2 teaspoons whole golden mustard seeds

Soak crumbs in half & half to soften. Lightly and thoroughly mix with pork, salt, sugar and thyme. Shape into 4 patties, each 1 1/4 inches thick. Heat about 2 tablespoons butter in a large heavy frying pan over medium heat until it bubbles well. Add patties and brown on both sides, about 10 minute total; turn occasionally. Arrange lettuce as a generously single layer liner for each patty on a serving plate. Place patties on lettuce. Remove from pan any excess fat or burned drippings. With pan off heat, add the remaining butter and the lemon juice and whisk or stir to blend quickly. Spoon over patties.

Note: Do not crowd patties in pan, add a little more butter during browning if needed. Each serving is a plump pork cushion on a tender base of mild lettuce. A small finishing of butter seasons both pork and lettuce. Accompany with boiled little new potatoes with skins. Serves 4.

Serve with 1985 Cabernet Reserve White, Edna Valley

Shirley Sarvis
The Chalone Wine Group

Lamb Chops with Spinach & Mushrooms

8 lamb chops
1/2 teaspoon minced rosemary
1/4 cup olive oil
1 1/2 teaspoon salt
1/2 cup Merlot 3

1 pound shiitake mushrooms, thickly sliced
1 pound spinach, rinsed and steamed
2 tablespoons unsalted butter

Preheat broiler or barbecue grill. Rub chops with 2 tablespoons olive oil, 1/2 teaspoon salt, and 1/4 teaspoon rosemary. Set aside. In large skillet, heat 1 tablespoon olive oil over high heat, add mushrooms, 1/2 teaspoon salt and 1/4 teaspoon rosemary. Cook until caramelized. Set aside. Broil chops about 5 inches from heat until golden on outside, rosy inside. About 3 minutes per side.

Reheat mushrooms, arrange down center of 4 plates, place 2 chops over the mushrooms. Keep warm. In large skillet, heat 1 tablespoon olive oil over medium heat. Add spinach and 1/2 teaspoon salt, cook to wilt. Spoon around chops.

Cover to keep warm. Add wine to spinach juices and cook over high heat until reduced to 1/4 cup. Reduce heat to low and add butter to thicken. Pour over chops and serve. Serves 4.

Gail Paquette, Chef
Belvedere Winery

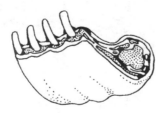

A Chardonnay Ham Glaze

3/4 cup grape juice
1/4 cup orange juice
1/2 cup raisins
zest of 1 chopped lemon
zest of 1 chopped orange
1 tablespoon cornstarch

1/2 cup Chardonnay
10 chopped dried apricots
1 ounce slivered almonds
dash of mace
dash of nutmeg
1/2 tablespoon Dijon mustard

In a sauce pan, simmer wine, grape and orange juice, raisins, and zest for 10 minutes until raisins are plumped and liquid starts to reduce. Add almonds and apricots. In a separate bowl, mix cornstarch, mustard, and 2 tablespoons cold water. Add slowly 3 tablespoons hot sauce. Mix well and return to pan. Cook, stirring for 1 minute. Add mace and nutmeg to taste. Makes 1 cup. Serve with finished ham.

Jill Davis, Winemaker
Buena Vista-Carneros Estate Winery

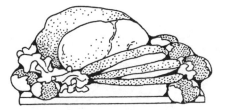

Lamb, Polenta & Pancetta Spiedinis

1 leg of lamb, trimmed, cut into
  1 inch cubes
1 cup olive oil
sage
rosemary
pancetta
Basalmic vinegar

3/4 gallon water
17 ounce bag instant polenta
4 tablespoons parsley, chopped
salt & pepper to taste
1 teaspoon sliced garlic
1 head radiccio

Marinate leg of lamb in 3/4 cup olive oil, sage, rosemary, 2 teaspoons sliced garlic, salt & pepper for 24 hours. Bring water and rest of ingredients except polenta to boil. Add polenta and simmer for 3 minutes. Pour onto greased sheet pan. Cool, and then cut into 1 inch cubes. Skewer lamb, polenta, lamb, polenta and so forth. Wrap pancetta around and secure on skewer. Brush with olive oil, salt and pepper. Grill to preferred doneness. Brush with oil again and serve over julienned radicchio that has been lightly tossed with Balsamic vinegar.

Wine: Sonoma Valley Zinfandel.

As served at the Sonoma Valley Vintners' Picnic in the Park.

Doug Lane
Ristoranti Piatti

Courtesy of the Sonoma Valley Cuisine Society.

Armenian Lamb Shanks with Pilaf

4 shanks, cleaned and fat trimmed
4 cloves chopped garlic
1 cup catsup
1 teaspoon Cayenne
1 cup chopped red pepper
1 cup chopped green pepper
1 leek (white only) sliced

2 cups chopped onions
2 cups chopped carrots
1 cup chopped celery
1 cup red wine
1/4 cup Worcestershire
1 teaspoon salt

Put shanks in a large heavy pot (large enough to have lamb shanks in single layer). Mix seasonings and vegetables. Pour over shanks and bake in a low 325° oven, covered for 2 to 4 hours. Scoop vegetables and sauce over lamb while cooking. When tender, place one shank on plate with extra sauce. Serve with rice pilaf and string beans. Serves 4.

PILAF:

2/3 cube butter
1/2 cup broken vermicelli
salt and pepper

2 cups water or chicken
  broth (broth is best)
1 cup long grain white rice

Melt butter in heavy skillet. Add vermicelli and stir until light brown. Add rice and stir until all rice is coated. Pour hot chicken broth over rice, stirring a few minutes. Bring to a boil and reduce heat to simmer. Add salt and pepper to taste. Cover tightly and simmer for 35 minutes. Remove lid, fluff with fork. Add currants and pine nuts (if desired). Serves 4.

Serve with Adler Fels Sobra Vista or Sangiacomo Chardonnay.

Adler Fels Winery

Adler Fels Winery owner Ayn Ryan Coleman has an Armenian heritage. A descendant of the Merzoian family, who emigrated to California from Bitlis, Armenia five generations ago, she keeps family tradition alive through the preparation of recipes that have been handed down from generation to generation.

Lamb Rack with Hazelnut Crust
with a Fig Cabernet Sauce

2 1/2 racks of lamb
1/3 cups hazelnuts, ground
2 tablespoons olive oil
2 tablespoons chopped fresh thyme

salt and pepper to taste
2 tablespoons chopped fresh
   rosemary

Prepare lamb racks. Combine hazelnuts and herbs with oil and press into meat. Season with salt and pepper. Cook racks by sauteing meat side down in olive oil until well browned. Place racks in 400° oven and cook for about 15-20 minutes. Allow to sit 5 minutes before slicing. While rack is cooking prepare sauce. Place lamb chops in pool of this sauce on individual plates. Garnish with fresh figs and fresh herbs.

CABERNET AND FIG DEMI-GLACE:

3 shallots, chopped fine
2 cloves garlic, chopped fine
1 cup Cabernet Sauvignon

1 quart strong lamb stock
4 dried figs, coarsely chopped
salt and pepper to taste

Put shallots and garlic and Cabernet in saucepan and reduce to about 1/4 cup. Add stock and reduce by half. Add figs. Continue to reduce until slightly thickened. Strain and keep warm until lamb is ready.

The wine: Our Alexander Valley Cabernet Sauvignon.

Rhonda Carano, Co-Owner
Ferrari-Carano Vineyards & Winery

Wine Country Brochettes

2 pounds boneless lamb,
  from shoulder or leg
1/2 cup Pinot Noir
1/4 cup olive oil
1/4 teaspoon ground black pepper

2 garlic cloves, slivered
1/2 teaspoon dried thyme
1/2 teaspoon dried rosemary
1/2 teaspoon salt

In a non-aluminum baking dish or bowl combine wine, oil, garlic with seasonings. Trim and cut lamb into 1-inch cubes. Add to marinade; marinate lamb at room temperature 2 to 4 hours, or cover and refrigerate up to 24 hours. Heat grill or broiler. If using wooden skewers, soak at least 15 minutes.

Thread lamb onto each of 8 wooden or metal skewers. Grill or broil, turning several times, about 10 minutes. 4 servings.

Wine: Charles Krug Pinot Noir.

Charlotte Walker, Chef
Charles Krug Winery

Mustard-Grilled Lamb Burgers

1 1/4 pounds extra-lean ground
  lamb
1 1/4 cups minced mushrooms
  (about 5 ounces)
1/2 cup chopped hazelnuts
  (filberts), chopped (about
  2 1/2 ounces)
1 clove garlic, minced or
  pressed

1 egg white, lightly beaten
1 teaspoon salt
1/4 teaspoon black pepper
vegetable oil for brushing
  on grill rack
mustard
8 hamburger buns, split
lettuce leaves

Combine the lamb, mushrooms, hazelnuts, garlic, egg white, salt and pepper in a medium-sized bowl. Divide the meat mixture into 8 equal portions and shape into round patties. In a grill with a cover, prepare a medium-hot fire for direct-heat cooking. Brush the grill rack with vegetable oil. Place the patties on the grill and cook, turning once, until done to your preference (5 to 8 minutes on each side). After turning, spread the tops of the patties with mustard. During the last few minutes of cooking, place the buns, cut side down, on the outer edges of the grill to toast lightly. Serve the burger and toasted buns with the Eggplant Salsa, Basil Yogurt, and lettuce for guests to assemble as desired. Serves 8.

BASIL YOGURT:

1/2 cup low-fat plain yogurt
2 tablespoons chopped fresh basil

1/2 cup sour cream

Combine the yogurt and basil in a blender or a food processor and blend well. Remove to a bowl and fold in the sour cream. Cover and chill.

EGGPLANT SALSA:

1 large eggplant, sliced
  crosswise 3/4 inch thick
1/4 cup olive oil
1/2 teaspoon chili powder
1 teaspoon salt
1 teaspoon ground cumin

1/2 small yellow onion,
  unpeeled
2 tablespoons diced canned
  roasted red pepper
1 tablespoon balsamic vinegar
  or red wine vinegar

Brush both sides of each eggplant slice with some of the olive oil. Combine the chili powder, salt and cumin and sprinkle both sides of the slices. Brush the grill rack with vegetable oil. Place the eggplant slices on the grill, cover and cook, turning once, until very brown on both sides. Meanwhile, brush the onion half with olive oil. Grill, covered, until the skin is crisp and blackened.

Remove eggplant and onion to a plate to cool. Slip off and discard the skins from the eggplant and onion, then chop coarsely. In a bowl, lightly combine the eggplant, onion, red pepper, and vinegar and set aside.

Serve Sutter Home Zinfandel with this interesting dish.

Sutter Home Winery

Good lamb recipes, other than the standard chops, roasts, etc. are not easily found, but this one is really good! Good enough to win $3,000 in Sutter Home's National Burger Cook-Off, for 2nd Prize.

Barbecued Lamb Kebabs
with Honey and Rosemary

1 pound lamb fillet, cut into
  1-inch cubes
8 large or 16 small mushrooms
1 lemon, sliced thickly
flowering rosemary, to garnish

1 orange, sliced thickly
4 tablespoons honey (rosemary,
  if possible)
2 teaspoons lavender flowers and
  leaves, mixed

Thread the lamb cubes, mushrooms (halve them if large), lemon, orange slices onto 4 skewers. Pour 1 tablespoon honey over each and leave to marinate with the lavender flowers and leaves for about one hour, turning the skewers occasionally, so that the kebabs are coated with honey. Heat the grill or barbecue until hot. Grill for 8-12 minutes, turning several times during cooking. Decorate each kebab with a sprig of flowering rosemary and serve with a lettuce salad dressed with walnut oil.

Suggested wine: Bandiera Cabernet Sauvignon.

Bandiera Winery

Spicy Sausage Burgers
with Roasted Pepper Relish

1 pound ground turkey
8 ounces andouille or other
  smoked spicy sausage, chopped

1 tablespoon chopped fresh
  thyme or 1 teaspoon dried
1/4 cup finely chopped red onion

In a grill with a cover, prepare a medium fire for direct heat cooking. Combine ingredients in a large bowl. Mix well. Divide the mixture into 4 equal portions and shape into oval patties about 1/2 inch thick.

RELISH:

1 large red bell pepper
2 fresh Anaheim or pasilla chile
  peppers
olive oil for brushing on
  vegetables on French rolls
2 tablespoons firmly packed
  brown sugar
4 sourdough French rolls, split

3/4 cup Zinfandel
1/2 cup chopped red onion
1 teaspoon minced fresh thyme
  or 1/4 teaspoon dried thyme
2 tablespoons cider vinegar
2 teaspoons Dijon mustard
vegetable oil for brushing on
  grill rack

Cut off the sides of the bell pepper forming 4 large slices in all. Cut the chilies in half lengthwise, remove and discard seeds. Brush the peppers and chilies with olive oil. Brush the grill rack with vegetable oil. Place the patties, pepper slices and chile halves on the grill. Cook patties, turning once, until juices run clear (5 to 7 minutes on each side). Grill peppers and chilies turning once until tender (4 to 5 minutes on each side).

Pour Zinfandel into a medium-sized saucepan and place on the grill rack. Bring to a boil and cook until reduced to 1 tablespoon. Remove from fire and stir in onion, thyme, vinegar, sugar and mustard. Peel the grilled peppers and chilies and cut into 1 inch long Julienne strips; add to the saucepan and mix well. Toast rolls lightly. Brush the cut sides of the rolls with olive oil. Place a burger on the bottom half of each roll. Spoon some pepper relish over the burgers and add the roll tops.

Wine selection: Sutter Home Zinfandel

Sutter Home Winery

It won the third prize of $2,000 in Sutter Home's National Burger cook-off.

Country Cactus Meatloaf

3/4 cups Sonoma dried tomato bits
1/4 cup yellow corn meal
3 large cloves, garlic, minced
3/4 cup boiling water
1 1/2 pound lean ground beef
2 eggs
2/3 cups sliced green onions
1 1/2 teaspoon salt

4 ounces diced mild green chilies
  (1 can)
1/3 cup chopped cilantro or
  parsley
2 medium fresh or canned
  jalapeno peppers, seeded and
  finely chopped
1/4 teaspoon pepper

In a large bowl mix tomato bits, corn meal, garlic and water. Set aside 10 minutes. Add remaining ingredients. Mix with hands or wooden spoon to blend thoroughly. In shallow baking pan or dish, form into a loaf about 12 inches by 4 inches. Sprinkle with about 1 tablespoon of additional corn meal. Bake in 375° oven 50-60 minutes - until juices run clear. Let stand 10 minutes before slicing. Serves 4 to 6.

Wine suggestion: Davis Bynum Barefoot Red

Timbercrest Farms

This meatloaf is quite different in flavor, texture and appearance.

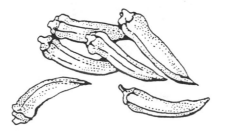

Mustard-Peppersteak

1-1 1/2 pounds boneless beef
steak (such as tenderloin,
fat trimmed)
2-3 teaspoons cracked black
pepper or to taste
1 1/2 teaspoons olive oil

1/4 cup brandy
2 teaspoons beef broth
2 tablespoons Cabernet
Sauvignon
1/2 cup gorgonzola or
crumbled blue cheese
1/2 teaspoon crumbled dry
tarragon

Slice beef tenderloin into 1" thick slices, about 2 1/4" to 2 1/2" round per slice (two slices per serving). Cover with about 1/4 to 1/2 teaspoon cracked pepper per slice (more pepper adds heat; don't overdo the pepper unless you want your steak hot). Heat a 10" skillet over medium high heat. Add oil to pan. Cook slices of beef until rich; brown on bottom, 3 1/2 to 4 minutes; turn over and cook to desired doneness (about 3 minutes, longer for medium rare).

Remove pan from heat, transfer meat to a plate, and set in warm oven to hold. Add 1/4 cup brandy to pan and scrape up cooked bits. Return pan to heat, add the beef broth and mustard, and reduce liquid by half, stirring to blend. Add the cheese and tarragon and stir until nearly blended (leave a little bit of chunkiness to the cheese). Remove from heat. Retrieve cooked tenderloin from oven, put individual portions on plates, and cover with sauce from pan. Or leave steak on serving platter, cover all the meat with the sauce and serve with a fork and spoon to ladle sauce over individual portions.

Garnish with a sprig of fresh tarragon if available. To give the dish added color and flavor, use a mix of peppers, such as cracked red and green peppercorns, with black pepper. Makes four servings.

Serve with William Wheeler R.S. Reserve or Cabernet Sauvignon

Ingrid Wheeler, Co-Owner
Wm. Wheeler Winery

Gamay Beaujolais Beef Stew

1/4 pound margarine
3 pounds cubed beef
2 cups beef broth
1 tablespoon flour
1 pound mushrooms
1 1/2 cups Gamay Beaujolais

6 medium onions
1 teaspoon salt
1/4 teaspoon pepper
1/2 teaspoon thyme
1/2 teaspoon marjoram

Saute onions in margarine. Brown meat on all sides and add to the onions. Add flour, salt, and spices, stirring until smooth. Add 1/2 cup broth and 1 cup Gamay Beaujolais. Add the remaining liquid during cooking time. Simmer 3 hours. Add mushrooms and continue cooking 1 hour. Serve over rice or noodles. Freezes well. Serves 6 to 8.

Wine: Gan Eden Gamay Beaujolais.

Frances R. Winchell
Gan Eden Wines

Napa Valley Basil-Smoked Burgers

2 pounds ground sirloin
1/4 cup Zinfandel
1/4 cup lightly packed minced
  fresh basil
1/4 cup minced red onion
1/4 cup fine fresh Italian
  bread crumbs
8 sun-dried tomatoes packed
  in oil, drained and finely
  chopped
1 to 2 teaspoons garlic salt
vegetable oil for brushing on
  grill rack

6 large seeded sandwich rolls,
  split
2/3 cup light mayonnaise
6 slices Monterey jack cheese
2 tablespoons prepared basil
  pesto
red leaf lettuce leaves
6 large tomato slices, about
  1/4" thick
paper-thin red onion rings
fresh basil sprigs (optional)
8 fresh basil sprigs moistened
  with water for tossing onto
  the fire

In a grill with a cover, prepare a medium-hot fire for direct-heat cooking. In a medium-sized bowl, lightly combine the sirloin, Zinfandel, minced basil, minced onion, bread crumbs, sun-dried tomatoes, and garlic salt to taste. Divide the meat mixture into 6 equal portions and shape into round patties. Brush the grill with vegetable oil. Toss the basil sprigs directly onto the coals, then place the patties on the grill and cook, turning once, until done to your preference (5 to 8 minutes on each side).

During the last minute or so of cooking, top each patty with a cheese slice. Meanwhile, in a small bowl, combine the mayonnaise and pesto. Spread the mixture on the cut sides of the toasted rolls. On the bottom half of each roll, layer the lettuce, burger, tomato slice, and onion ring. Add basil sprigs, if desired, and roll tops. Serves 6.

You'll enjoy Sutter Home Zinfandel with these burgers.

Sutter Home Winery

This recipe was the Grand Prize Winner in a national competition by Sutter Home. It won $10,000. It deserved it ... a great recipe, and well worth the effort!

Quick Chili a la Burgundy

2 15-1/4 ounce cans of kidney
  beans
2 medium cans chopped tomatoes
1 pound ground chuck
1 large onion
1 clove garlic

1/2 red pepper
1/2 green pepper
Tabasco to taste
chili powder to taste
2 cups Burgundy

Drain juice from kidney beans and save. Refill cans with wine just to cover beans, let stand. Meanwhile, saute garlic, onion, chopped peppers and add ground chuck. Add tomatoes, kidney beans with wine, original juice and seasonings. Simmer 1-2 hours or in crock pot on low for 2-4 hours. Serves 4 to 6.

Serve with Martini & Prati Burgundy.

Jeani Martini
Martini & Prati Wines

Blue Cheese Burgers

2 pounds lean ground beef
4 tablespoons Cabernet Sauvignon
2 garlic cloves, minced
1 teaspoon salt
1/2 teaspoon ground black pepper

4 ounces blue cheese
1/3 cup chopped walnuts
1 long baguette
olive oil
chopped parsley

Combine beef, wine, garlic, salt and pepper. Shape meat into 12 oval patties. Mash cheese and blend with walnuts. Divide cheese mixture equally onto centers of 6 patties. Top with remaining patties, pinching edges together to seal in filling. Place on a baking sheet and bake at 500° for 10-12 minutes to desired doneness (or pan fry or charcoal grill burgers). Cut baguette into 6 pieces; split each piece and paint with olive oil. Place on baking sheet and toast at 500° 3-4 minutes. Sprinkle burgers with chopped parsley. 6 servings.

Wine Selection: Charles Krug Cabernet Sauvignon

Charlotte Walker, Consulting Chef
Charles Krug Winery

SEAFOOD

Scallops with Red Pepper Sauce

1 pound scallops, slice if large
2 large avocados, sliced

Marinate scallops in lime or lemon juice until opaque, about 3 to 4 hours.

RED PEPPER SAUCE:

4 red peppers, roasted & peeled
2 tablespoons raspberry vinegar

2 tablespoons extra virgin olive
oil
salt & pepper to taste

Blend above ingredients in a food processor or blender. Add additional oil or vinegar if desired. Season to taste. Refrigerate until ready to serve.

To serve: Place a pool of the sauce in a serving dish. Arrange scallops and avacado slices in an attractive pattern on the sauce. Serves 6.

Serve with Sauvignon Blanc.

Bettina Dreyer, Vice President
Grand Cru Vineyards

Spicy Lobster Risotto
with a Fried Leek Julienne

3 Maine lobsters, cut and sauteed
  briefly in olive oil and shelled
6 ounces tomato concasee,
  peeled and seeded
1 pound Beretta risotto, superfino
  Arborio
1/2 medium yellow onion, chopped
salt and Cayenne pepper to taste

2 quarts chicken stock
2 ounces "Regiano" Parmesan,
  freshly grated
1 1/2 ounce olive oil
3 ounces sweet butter
4 leaves fresh sage
2 sprigs fresh thyme
1 leek

In a large stock pot, heat olive oil over medium high heat. Add onions, sage and thyme. Cook for 3 minutes and stir with a wood spatula so the onions do not color. Add risotto and cook another 2 minutes, continuing to stir. Add boiling chicken stock 2 ounces at a time. Cook risotto for about 10 minutes until "al dente."

Add lobster, tomato, Cayenne pepper and Parmesan. Continue to cook, while stirring the entire time until risotto is "al dente" and creamy. Finish by adding sweet butter or lobster butter. Cut leek in half length-wise, wash under cold running water. Cut the white and light green of the leek in two 2" pieces. With a chef's knife, julienne the leek. Dust with a little flour and fry on medium heat until julienne gets a little crispy, do not color. Drain on a paper towel, light salt and keep warm.

Adjust seasonings of the risotto and divide onto 6 soup plates. Garnish the top with a pinch of fried leek julienne. Serve immediately. Serves 6. This risotto should have the sweetness of the lobster, a little of the heat from the Cayenne pepper, and the crunchiness of the leeks.

This delectable dish marries perfectly with Chandon Blanc de Noirs.

Philippe Jeanty, Chef de Cuisine
Domaine Chandon

Curried Lobster and Mushroom Tartlets

2 tablespoons sweet butter
1/4 cup finely chopped onion
1 1/2 teaspoons curry powder
1/4 pound chanterelle or hedge
  hog mushrooms or 6 ounces
  standard commercial mushrooms

1/2 cup heavy cream
1 teaspoon cornstarch
1 tablespoon cornstarch
1 tablespoon Chardonnay
1 cup chopped, cooked lobster
  (about 6 ounces)*

In a heavy saucepan heat the butter and saute the onion without browning over medium low heat until translucent. Add the curry powder and saute for a few seconds to release the flavors. Add the cream. Dissolve cornstarch in wine and stir into cream. Bring to a boil, stirring frequently, then simmer slowly until the sauce is very thick.

Clean and chop the mushrooms. In a large skillet heat the remaining tablespoon of butter and when very hot add the mushrooms. Saute until mushrooms are lightly browned and tender. Add to the curry sauce along with salt. Simmer a minute a two, then add lobster. Taste and add more salt if required.

If you're ready to fill the tartlet shells, cook just until lobster is heated through. Otherwise remove from heat and set aside until needed. Can be refrigerated for two days. Reheat quickly, stirring frequently as overcooking will destroy the lobster's delicate flavor and texture. Fill the tartlet shells and serve.

PASTRY:**

6 ounces sweet butter, chilled
1 1/2 cups all-purpose flour

1/4 teaspoon salt
3-4 tablespoons cold Chardonnay

Cut the chilled butter into pieces and combine with flour and salt in a bowl or food processor. Process until mixture is mealy. Add 3 tablespoons wine and pulse a few times. Transfer to a bowl and finish blending by hand, adding more wine only if necessary to hold dough together. Form dough into a ball, wrap in plastic wrap and refrigerate for at least 1/2 hour to relax gluten before rolling.

Dough can be made up to 3 days in advance and refrigerated. Roll out dough quite thin on a lightly floured board. Cut into circles and fit into small tartlet tins or miniature muffin pans, pressing in well. Prick with fork.

Gather up remaining dough and roll out again.

Refrigerate at least 20 minutes before baking. Bake in a preheated 425° oven for about 15 minutes or until nicely browned. After 5 minutes if pastry seems to be puffing too much, push down gently with back of a teaspoon, otherwise you may not have a shell to fit. The tartlets are best when baked no more than an hour or two in advance.

*If you don't want to deal with a whole lobster, buy a lobster tail and steam it. Cooked crab would also work well in this recipe.

**If you prefer something simpler to prepare, use one of these alternatives to making the pastry tarts.

TOAST CASES:

| 24 slices commercial "thin-sliced" bread | 2 tablespoons butter |

Cut bread into rounds with a cutter. Melt butter and brush bread rounds generously. Brush small tartlet tins or miniature muffin pans with butter. Press bread rounds into pans firmly. Bake in 425° oven for about 6 minutes or until nicely browned. Remove toast cases from pans and cool on a rack. The cases will crisp as they cool. Should any seems moist, return to the hot oven for a minute. Can be made an hour or two in advance.

MELBA TOASTS:

| 12 slices commercial "thin-sliced" bread | 2 tablespoons butter |

Stack bread slices and trim off crusts. Cut slices in half on the diagonal to make 24 triangles. Melt butter and brush triangles generously. Brush a baking sheet with butter and place triangles on it. Bake in 425° oven until gold n brown - about 5 minutes. Remove from oven. When cool, the toasts should be crisp and dry, if moist return to oven for another minute. The toasts can be made several hours in advance.

Wine: 1987 Sterling Vineyards Diamond Mountain Chardonnay.

Richard Alexei, Wine & Food Consultant
Sterling Vineyards

Chardonnay Shrimp

1/2 cup butter or margarine
2 garlic cloves, minced
1 cup Chardonnay
1 teaspoon Worcestershire sauce
teaspoon salt
1/2 teaspoon dried leaf thyme

1/2 teaspoon dried leaf oregano
1/4-1/2 teaspoons crushed hot
  red pepper flakes
1 1/2 pound unpeeled medium-1/2
  size shrimp, rinsed and drained
2 tablespoons finely chopped
  parsley

Melt butter in a large skillet over medium heat. Add garlic; cook 1 minute. Stir in Chardonnay, Worcestershire sauce and seasonings; bring to a boil. Add shrimp, simmer 4 to 5 minutes until firm and pink, stirring frequently. Sprinkle with parsley. Serve with cooking juices. 4 servings.

Wine selection: Charles Krug Chardonnay

Charlotte Walker, Consulting Chef
Charles Krug Winery

Finger food at its finest: shrimp are left in shells - messier to eat, but fun and tasty - and easier on the cook. Serve with plenty of French bread to sop up the juices.

Butterfly Shrimp in the Oven

30 fresh jumbo shrimp
1/4 cup olive oil
3/4 cup toasted bread crumbs
pinch salt
pinch black pepper
pinch crushed red pepper

2 large garlic cloves, crushed
10 fresh parsley sprigs, leaves
 only
6 tablespoons melted butter
1/4 cup grated Parmesan cheese

Preheat oven to 300°. Slit the shrimps down the back, but leave the shells on. Devein, wash and dry thoroughly. Arrange the shrimps in an oiled ovenproof dish. Pour olive oil evenly over them. Sprinkle bread crumbs, salt and pepper over them. Chop parsley and garlic together, sprinkle over the shrimps and stir gently to mix. Cover the pan with foil and bake for 20 minutes. Remove the foil, spoon butter over the shrimps and bake uncovered for about 5 minutes longer. Check for doneness.

Sprinkle with cheese before serving. May be served with spaghettini al burro. Serve the pasta on the same plate with shrimps, spooning juices over the spaghettini. Top with grated cheese. Serves 8-10.

Our barrel fermented Chardonnay makes a delightful accompaniment to this.

Elaine Wellesley, Winemaker
Quail Ridge Cellars & Vineyards

Navajo Spiced Prawns in
Red Pepper Vinaigrette

juice of 1 lime
1/3 cup olive oil
2 teaspoons chopped fresh
cilantro leaves
2 teaspoons chopped fresh
oregano or 1 teaspoon dried
2 teaspoons chopped fresh
chives

2 teaspoons mild chili powder
salt & pepper to taste
32 prawns, peeled, butterflied
(do not cut through)
2 to 3 tablespoons olive oil
red pepper vinaigrette (see recipe)
2 teaspoons ground cumin

THE DAY BEFORE SERVING: Combine lime juice, 1/3 cup olive oil, cilantro, cumin, oregano, chives, chile powder, salt and pepper, for marinade. Add prawns to marinade; marinate in refrigerator overnight, turning prawns occasionally. WHEN READY TO SERVE: Remove prawns from marinade, discarding marinade. Lightly saute prawns in 2 to 3 tablespoons olive oil until they lose their transparency. Serve prawns on a bed of red pepper vinaigrette. 8 Servings.

VINAIGRETTE:

3 large red bell peppers
1 clove garlic, finely chopped
1 tablespoon Balsamic vinegar

2/3 cup extra-virgin olive oil
salt & pepper to taste

Roast peppers under broiler or over gas flame until skin is blackened. Place peppers in paper bag to steam for 10 minutes. Under cold running water, scrape blackened skin from peppers. Remove and discard stems and seeds. In food processor or blender, puree peppers and garlic. With machine running, add vinegar, 1/2 teaspoon salt and olive oil. Season to taste with salt and pepper.

Wine: Chateau Souverain Sauvignon Blanc

Patricia Windisch,
Executive Chef/General Manager
Chateau Souverain Restaurant

Mussels Steamed Over Tomato and Basil

36 medium mussels
  (about 2 1/2 pounds)
3 tablespoons olive oil
2 cloves garlic, sliced thin
dash crushed red pepper (optional)
freshly ground black pepper

1/4 cup loosely packed finely
  shredded basil
1 cup drained Italian plum
  tomatoes, diced (1/4 inch)
kosher salt

Rinse the mussels under cold running water. Scrub the shells thoroughly and pull out the "beard," the wiry substance that protrudes from between the flat sides of the mussel shell. Drain thoroughly. Heat the oil in a large deep skillet over medium heat. Stir in the basil and fry until bright green, a few seconds. Carefully stir in the tomatoes, sprinkle with salt and reduce to low heat. Simmer just until the tomatoes are softened and begin to release their liquid, about 3 minutes.

Season to taste with salt and pepper. Add mussels. Cover and steam, shaking the pan occasionally, until mussels open, about 4 minutes. Spoon some mussels and cooking liquid into serving bowls. Serves 6.

Suggested wine: St. Supéry 1989 Sauvignon Blanc.

St. Supéry Vineyards & Winery

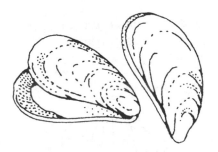

Barbecued Oysters

Barbecued oysters need no elaborate preparation. Just grill the oysters, cut side down, so they cook in their own juice. Don't turn them during cooking. They are done when shells open, about 6-8 minutes. Serve on the half shell with either of these sauces.

CILANTRO CHUTNEY:

1 cup cilantro
4 green onions roughly chopped
1 tablespoon lemon juice
1/4 teaspoon ground cinnamon
1/4 teaspoon ground cumin

2 small hot green chilies
  (serrano or jalepeno)
1/4 teaspoon ground tumeric
1/4 teaspoon ground cloves
salt & pepper to taste

Process all ingredients in food processor or blender until a smooth paste forms. Add more lemon juice or a little water to desired consistency.

EAST MEETS OYSTERS SALSA:

1/4 cup fresh ginger, peeled
  and shredded
3 spring onions, finely chopped
1/2 cup rice wine vinegar

splash of sesame oil
zest of 1 orange
squeeze of lemon juice
salt & pepper to taste

Mix all ingredients together. Let stand several minutes before using.

Serve with Frogs Leap Sauvignon Blanc.

Beverly Salinger, Resident Chef
Frog's Leap Winery

Scallops and Prawns
with Sun-Dried Apricots, Mint and Yogurt

8 fresh large prawns, peeled and devained

8-12 ounces of fresh bay scallops

6-9 pieces (approximately 2 tablespoons) Julienned sun-dried apricots

4 tablespoons plain low fat yogurt

2 good pinches of fresh chopped mint

1-2 ounces Muscat wine

Using only 1/3 teaspoon olive oil, saute the prawns. When it is time to turn the prawns, add scallops and toss. Add the apricots and mint, cook until the scallops are just beginning to change from translucent to opaque. Be very careful not to over-cook. Add the wine and the yogurt and stir gently. Remove from the heat and carefully extract the seafood from the sauce, then return the sauce to a low flame for a moment or two, until the sauce reduces slightly. Add the seafood and toss lightly. Serve with steamed vegetables and natural brown rice.

Stephen Meyer, Chef
The Willetts' Brewing Company

Stephen Meyer, a very innovative chef and a contributor to several other cookbooks, is now responsible for the cuisine at this brewhouse and restaurant.

Swordfish with Basil-Mustard Butter

6 swordfish steaks
1 cup Fumé or Sauvignon Blanc
salt & pepper to taste

Preheat oven to 350°. Arrange swordfish in a single layer in aaking dish. Pour wine around the fish to a depth equal to half the thickness of the steaks. Set the dish in the middle of the oven and bake for 9 minutes. Check doneness with a fork. Transfer to heated plates and spoon the Basil-Mustard butter on to the center of each steak. Serve immediately. Serves 6.

BASIL-MUSTARD BUTTER:

1 stick sweet butter
1/4 cup Dijon butter
1/4 cup chopped fresh basil

Combine all ingredients until smooth.

Serve with our 1987 Fumé Blanc or 1988 Sauvignon Blanc.

Mrs. Mitsuko Shrem
Clos Pegase Winery

Tuna with Lavender

3 pounds fresh tuna, cut in
  1" slices
2 tablespoons whole black
  peppercorns
2 tablespoons Szechuan
  peppercorns
2 tablespoons fresh or 4
  tablespoons dried lavender
  flowers and/or buds*

2 tablespoons olive oil
2 tablespoons butter
3 tablespoons minced shallots
1 cup chicken stock
1 cup Cabernet Sauvignon
4 tablespoons softened butter

Crush peppercorns with pestle, or process with steel blade in food processor. Mix pepper with lavender and press into both sides of the tuna slices. Cover and let stand at least 1/2 hour, up to 3 hours for maximum pepper flavor. Sear over high heat in butter and oil 3-4 minutes on each side. (This is a dish that can be served rare. Check for desired doneness by piercing with the point of a small, sharp knife.)

Hold fish in a warm oven while making the sauce. Add shallots to saute pan and cook about 1 minute. Deglaze the pan with the stock, then add the Cabernet and cook rapidly until reduced by half. Remove pan from heat and stir in butter. Pour sauce over tuna and serve immediately. Serves 6.

Suggested wine: Simi Cabernet Sauvignon

*Dried lavender is available in many health food stores.

Mary Evely, Chef
Simi Winery

Grilled Tuna with Papaya Slices

4 medium-size tuna steaks
1 papaya, peeled, seeded and
  diced into small cubes
1 small red onion, diced
freshly ground pepper

2 tablespoons fresh cilantro
  coarsely chopped
1 tablespoon olive oil, plus
  olive oil to brush on tuna
juice of 2 limes

An hour before serving, toss together papaya, onion, cilantro, lime juice, olive oil and pepper. Cover and keep at room temperature. Brush tuna steaks with olive oil. Grill over hot coals, 3 to 4 minutes per side until pink in center. Top with salsa and serve. Serves 4.

Serve with Pine Ridge Chardonnay, Knollside Cuvee.

Nancy F. Andrus, Co-Owner
Pine Ridge Winery

Stuffed Trout

4 fresh trout, boned
8 ounces feta cheese
2 tablespoons chives, chopped
2 tablespoons Sonoma dried
  tomato bits

Black pepper to taste
1/4 cup water
1/4 cup dry white wine
  (Fume Blanc or Sauvignon
  Blanc)

Lay trout aside. Mix remaining ingredients in a small bowl, breaking up large chunks of cheese, using water and wine to moisten the mixture. Stuff each trout with 1/4 of the mixture. Pin together open ends of trout with toothpicks. Place in baking dish and bake at 400° for 20 minutes, turning once, until flesh is opaque and flakes with a fork. Serve with more of whatever wine was used in the stuffing.

Waltenspiel Kitchens
Timbercrest Farms

Fillets Sealed in Silver

4 lean white fish filets or salmon
  fillets (5 to 8 ounces each)
salt & pepper to taste
1/4 cup Sauvignon Blanc
3/4 teaspoon dried dill weed

1 large (or 2 slender) green
  onion with green top
1 teaspoon finely grated lemon
  zest
2 tablespoons butter or
  margarine, cut in small pieces

Preheat oven to 475°. Tear off 4 pieces of aluminum foil, about 12 inches long. Rinse fillets; pat dry with paper towels. Season both sides with salt and pepper. Place one fillet on each piece of foil. Spoon 1 tablespoon wine over each fillet. Finely chop green onion; reserve green part for garnish. Scatter white onion, lemon zest and dill over fillets. Dot with butter. Fold foil, sealing fillets in packets. Place on baking sheets. Bake 8 to 12 minutes, depending on thickness of fillets. Transfer fish out of foil to serving plates. Garnish with chopped green onion tops. 4 servings.

To accompany this, our Sauvignon Blanc.

Charlotte Walker
Charles Krug Winery

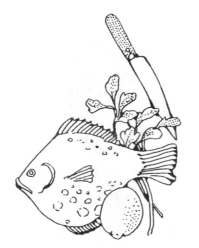

Salmon Baked in Foil Parcel
with Spring or Summer Flowers

2 ounces (1/4 cup) butter, softened
1 5-6 pound fresh salmon, cleaned
flowers in season*
1/2 cup well-flavored fish stock

1/4 cup Chardonnay
melted butter
black pepper

Heat the oven to 300°. Spread butter over the salmon and place flowers on top. Put salmon on a large piece of buttered foil and pour over the fishstock and wine. Fold the foil over the salmon and seal the edges to make a parcel. Place on baking sheet and bake in the oven allowing 12 minutes per pound. Carefully unwrap the salmon and serve on an oval dish, garnished with seasonal flowers. Serves 12. Serve the salmon with melted butter, black pepper and fresh flowers.

*If cooking the salmon in spring, use Parma violets, English cowslips or chive flowers. If you wait until summer, use squash flowers, pink and red clover blossoms.

Serve with Bandiera Chardonnay.

Bandiera Winery

Poached Fillet of Salmon, Oysters and Chives

2 6 ounce salmon fillets
1 teaspoon chopped shallots
1/2 cup Chardonnay
2 teaspoons chopped chives (a)
8 oysters, shells scrubbed
salt and white pepper

1/2 cup heavy cream
3/4 cube butter, unsalted
2 teaspoons chopped chives (b)
1 cup julienne carrots, leeks,
  jicama, lightly blanched

Season salmon with salt and white pepper. Use a little of the butter to grease bottom of a pan. Sprinkle on this, the shallots and chives (a), and place salmon on top. Pour in the white wine and heat until just begins to boil. Add the oysters in the shells and cover pan with aluminum foil. Simmer for 4 minutes and remove from heat. Remove salmon and oysters. Oysters will be open. Remove upper shell from 4, and entire shell from other four.

Replace the cooking liquor onto high heat and reduce by half. Add the heavy cream and continue to reduce until the sauce begins to thicken. Remove from the heat and vigorously whisk in the remaining butter; season to taste remembering that the salt water from the oysters may already have given enough salt. Place the salmon on plates.

Place the two oysters without shells on top of each fillet and pour over the sauce. Make a small nest of the vegetables on each plate and place on top of each two of the oysters in the half shell. Sprinkle with the chopped chives (b) and serve.

Serve with Black Mountain Vineyard Chardonnay.

Christina Tate,
J.W. Morris Winery

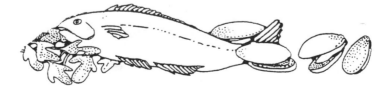

123

Saumon Sauvignon
(Salmon in Puff Pastry)

2 puff pastry sheets, frozen
2 pounds salmon filets, skinless
3 eggs, hard boiled

1 bunch fresh (or frozen) spinach
1 bunch fresh dill
egg wash (50/50 egg & water)

Place thawed (but still cold) pastry shell on ungreased baking pan. Layer salmon filet, minced dill, boiled and drained spinach, minced hard boiled eggs. Salt and pepper to taste. Brush egg wash along edges of pastry. Cover with second pastry sheet and press edges together with the tines of a fork. Brush egg wash over top shell. Bake 20 minutes at 400° pre-heated oven. Remove from oven and loosen pan with spatula. Slice and serve on maltese sauce. Serves 4.

MALTESE SAUCE:

(A Hollandaise Sauce with Fresh Orange Juice)

4 egg yolks
1/2 pound butter, clarified
1 orange
1 lemon wedge

4 ounces white wine
(Sauvignon Blanc)
white pepper
tabasco

Place 4 egg yolks in a mixing bowl, preferably stainless steel. Allow the yolks to come to room temperature. Clarify 1/2 pound of butter and allow to come to room temperature. Place the bowl over a simmering pot of water but do not let the water touch the bowl. While whipping the egg yolks, slowly trickle the butter into the yolks. Do not allow the eggs to thicken to a scrambled egg consistency by adding equal parts of the juice of one orange and white wine. Squeeze in the juice of one lemon wedge and a few dashes of tabasco. Salt and white pepper to taste. Whip the sauce till it has the consistency of fresh whipped cream. Ladle onto a dinner plate and place the Saumon Sauvignon on the sauce.

Serve with St. Supéry Sauvignon Blanc.

St. Supéry Vineyards & Winery

Salmon Chardonnay

whole salmon
salt & pepper to taste
Bermuda onions

2 or 3 sprigs fresh fennel
1 1/2 cups Chardonnay
unpeeled lemon

Scale and wash whole salmon, pat dry, salt and pepper both sides and place on rack in fish poacher. Cover top with alternating thin slices of Bermuda onions and unpeeled lemon. Add 2 or 3 sprigs of fresh fennel. Pour over 1 1/2 cups Chardonnay, cover tightly and cook at 350°, allowing about 6 minutes per pound. Baste frequently with the Chardonnay.

To serve, lift from poacher on rack, transfer to platter, and garnish with lemon quarters and fresh parsley. Before slicing, remove onion and lemon slices and fennel, and cut 1 inch to 2 inch slices just to bone. When top of fish is served and bone exposed, remove it carefully and continue slicing. With it you may pass a sauce made of two parts mayonnaise to one part prepared sour cream with a sprinkling of finely chopped dill and parsley.

With the salmon we like small red potatoes boiled in their skins, fresh asparagus, sour dough bread, and of course Caswell Vineyards Chardonnay.

Helen Caswell, Owner
Caswell Winter Creek Farm and Vineyards

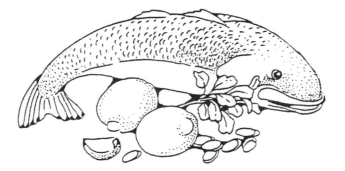

Grilled Salmon with
Orange-Saffron Butter

6 salmon steaks (1 inch thick)
vegetable oil
salt & pepper to taste

Heat grill. Brush fish with oil and season with salt and pepper. Grill on each side for 4-5 minutes.

SAUCE:

5 tablespoons butter	1 tablespoon orange zest
1/4 teaspoons saffron	2 teaspoons chopped shallots
1 tablespoon orange juice	salt and pepper to taste

Dissolve saffron in the orange juice. Place all ingredients into a food processor or blender and puree. Sauce may be prepared in advance and stored in the refrigerator for up to a week. Serve salmon with a dollop of saffron butter, Juliened summer vegetables, and Franciscan Oakville Estate Chardonnay. Serves 6.

Franciscan Vineyards, Inc.

Easy Poached Salmon

4 salmon steaks, 1/2-3/4" thick	1 teaspoon salt
1/2 cup Chenin Blanc	1 1/2 cups hot water
or Chardonnay	1 lemon (sliced)
2 peppercorns	1 teaspoon minced onion
1 bay leaf	

Suitable flat container for microwave. Cook everything except salmon in microwave on high for 5 minutes. Remove from microwave and lay 4 salmon steaks in broth. Cover with wax paper. Cook on high 1 minute per side. Let it sit in oven for 5 minutes. Serves 4.

Serve with Gan Eden Chenin Blanc or Chardonnay.

Frances R. Winchell
Gan Eden Wines

Salmon Kebabs

8 salmon steaks
6 red and/or green bell peppers
24 large fresh mushrooms

24 small boiling or pearl onions
24 small Roma tomatoes (or
 cherry tomatoes)

Remove skin and bones from salmon steaks and cut into 2 inch cubes. Clean peppers and cut into 2 inch squares. Trim stems from mushrooms. Peel onions. Using skewers, make kebabs by alternating salmon, pepper, mushroom, onion, and tomato. Lay kebabs in one layer in shallow pan. Pour marinade (see below) over kebabs and refrigerate 8 hours. Turn the kebabs occasionally. Grill over medium fire and baste with the marinade. We use seasoned grape cuttings for the fire (they burn, very hot), but you can use your favorite wood or charcoal.

MARINADE:

2 cups virgin olive oil
1 cup Chardonnay
4 ounces fresh lemon or lime
 juice

1/4-1/3 cup fresh lemon thyme,
 fresh oregano, or fresh
 cilantro, coarsely chopped
salt & pepper to taste

Mix ingredients. Making the marinade with lemon thyme and lemon juice gives a California (or Provencal) style; cilantro and lime juice - Latin American; and oregano and lemon juice - Greek.

Our Napa Valley Chardonnay is suggested.

Chateau Montelena Winery

127

Cold Poached Salmon

1 5-7 pound gutted fish with head and tail on and gills removed

2 cups dry white wine

2 onions, peeled and finely sliced

2 carrots, washed and sliced

1 stalk celery, washed and sliced

2 tablespoons whole peppercorns

2 tablespoons salt

3 bay leaves

enough water to half fill the poacher

Poaching the whole fish with skin intact retains the juices. You will need a deep fish poacher at least 24 inches long, with a lid and a rack that rests on the bottom with long handles for lifting out the fish. Or you may use a long roasting pan if it is deep enough for the poaching liquid to cover fish. In place of a rack you may wrap the fish in several layers of cheesecloth for lifting the fish out of the liquid. Place the poacher over two heating units on the stove top. Bring to a boil and simmer 1 hour. Poach your fish a day ahead, since it will have to be chilled in the poaching liquid overnight. Cooking time will be figured by thickness rather than weight. So measure width of the fish at its thickest part. Rinse the cavity of the fish well and be sure the red vein along the inner backbone (actually the fish's kidneys) is removed.

Slide the fish into the poacher on its side. Add enough boiling water so that the fish is just covered by the poaching liquid. Set the heat on high and when the water returns to the boil, lower heat so that the water barely boils in the covered poacher. For fish to be served hot, figure 15 minutes for every inch of thickness. Reduce to 13 minutes for fish to be served cold, since it will be cooled in the hot poaching liquid, and will continue to cook after being removed from the stove. Cooling the fish in the bouillon retains the juices, and once the fish his cold, the juice congeals since it contains gelatin. The finished product is very moist, and retains its shape well.

When the fish is cooked, cool it in the poacher, uncovered to room temperature, then refrigerate overnight. Lift the cold fish out of the poaching liquid, and allow to drain. Slide it gently from the rack on to the serving platter. With a sharp knife, trim through the skin along the sides of the gill plates and along the backbone, and peel the skin away, trimming a neat curve where it joins to the tail. Gently scrape away any brown meat on the sides until only pink is showing.

DECORATING COLD FISH:

black olives   Fresh dill sprigs or sliced
cooked carrot slices (from   unpeeled cucumber
  bouillon)

Cover the now unsightly eye with a small circle of cooked carrot and a slightly smaller piece of black olive. Dipping these in the aspic will "glue them" in place. Garnish the side very simply with fresh tarragon dill or strips of green leek. Blanch them first: put into boiling water (40 seconds for leek, 15 for tarragon, 5 for dill); then cool under cold water and drain. Dip any piece of decoration into the warm aspic so it will say in place on the cold fish.

ASPIC COATING:

1/2 cup water   3 cups poaching bouillon
5 envelopes unflavored gelatin ice cubes

Soften gelatin in water in a pot for several minutes. Carefully ladle 3 cups of bouillon from the upper portion of the poacher (to avoid sediment from the bottom) and strain through cheese cloth in the pot with the gelatin mixture. Heat to a simmer, remove from heat and let stand while you decorate the fish. Then put the pot containing the aspic into a large bowl, and surround it with ice cubes. Add some cold water to just cover the ice.

With a ladle or large spoon, stir the aspic slowly; it will thicken as it cools. When it is somewhat thicker than heavy cream you must very rapidly (in 5 seconds or so) ladle it on the fish in long smooth strokes from head to tail. The aspic continues to thicken and will become lumpy if not used quickly enough. If there are a few lumps, you may heat the blade of a wooden handled knife in a gas flame, and smooth them out.

BAKED SALMON TO BE SERVED COLD:

A very satisfactory alternative to poaching the fish is to bake it in tin foil. You can place the fish on its stomach on a bed of finely sliced onion, curving it in the foil and against the sides of the pan. Pour in a cup of dry white wine and 3 tablespoons butter. I prop the fish's mouth open by inserting a broken toothpick upright inside. Tuck some springs of fresh dill, sorrel or tarragon around the sides, and squeeze a lemon over the whole thing. Seal in foil until it is completely enclosed and bake at 325°.

The cooked fish will remain in this position when served, and will look as if it is swimming. This works for a fish too long to be placed on its side in any pan that you have, and it is stunning. The disadvantage here is that it is much harder to scrape off the dark layer of fat along the sides of the cooked and cooled salmon, and I don't bother.

For a fish (and pan) too large for the refrigerator, I put it in the bathtub, and surround it with four bags of ice and some cold water. When the fish is chilled, ease it onto a serving platter and peel away all of the foil and cooked vegetables. Skin and glaze the fish, as above, but it needs no decoration aside from covering the eyes. Place fresh dill springs or lines of unpeeled cucumber slices along the sides, and garnish with some cooked crayfish fleeing from the gorgeous monster.

HERB SAUCE FOR COLD FISH:

1/4 pint plain yogurt	1/4 cup fresh parsley, chopped
1/4 pint sour cream	1/4 cup fresh tarragon or dill,
1/4 pint homemade mayonnaise	chopped
juice of 1 lemon	1 shallot, minced

This is a pleasant change from mayonnaise. Combine the mayonnaise, lemon juice and shallot and beat well. Stir in the sour cream and yogurt. Fold in the herbs.

One of our Chardonnays goes well with this dish.

Barbara Winiarski, Co-Owner
Stag's Leap Wine Cellars

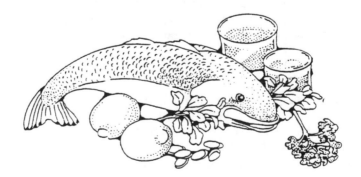

Salmon Poached in Champagne and Cream Sauce with Fresh Papaya

2 cups Champagne or sparkling
 wine
2 cups heavy whipping cream
2 tablespoons unsalted butter

4-6 ounce salmon filets
1 papaya, peeled, seeded &
 quartered

Put Champagne in skillet large enough to hold the salmon filets. Bring to a boil and reduce by half. Add cream and return to boil. Simmer salmon in mixture for 5 minutes. Place a papaya quarter, which has been cut into a fan, on top of each filet and continue to cook until the salmon is done, about 3 more minutes. It should be firm to touch but still moist in the center. Remove salmon from pan and keep warm. Reduce sauce to about 1 or 1-1/4 cups. Whisk in 2 tablespoons of butter and pour over salmon. Serves 4.

Wine recommendation: Benziger of Glen Ellen Blanc de Blancs.

Stella Fleming, Executive Chef
Glen Ellen Winery

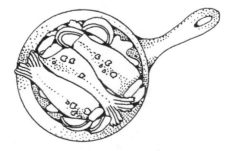

POULTRY

Royal Quail

6 whole quail, cleaned
1 cup wild rice, cooked
1 tablespoon chopped truffles

2 tablespoons melted butter
salt & pepper to taste

Mix 1 cup cooked wild rice with 2 tablespoons melted butter and 1 tablespoon finely chopped truffles. Divide the stuffing between 6 cleaned whole quail. Brush the birds with melted butter and season with salt and pepper. Roast in preheated oven at 450° for 15-20 minutes until richly browned. Serve with Cabernet Sauvignon sauce (see below) on the side and accompany with baby asparagus, steamed spinach or chicory.

CABERNET SAUVIGNON SAUCE:

2 shallots, finely chopped
2 tablespoons butter
1 cup Cabernet Sauvignon

2 cups chicken stock
1 black truffle, finely chopped

Gently saute the shallots in 1 tablespoon of the butter without browning. Add Cabernet and cook over high heat until reduced to about 1/2 cup. Add chicken stock and continue cooking over high heat until reduced to 1 cup. Stir in truffle and rest of butter. Keep warm until quail are roasted.

Rich and succulent, this dish is ideally accompanied by our Quail Ridge Cabernet Sauvignon. Serves 6.

Elaine Wellesley, Winemaker
Quail Ridge Cellars & Vineyards

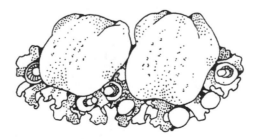

Smoked Chicken Tamales
With a Smoky Corn Salsa

TAMALE DOUGH:

2/3 cup pork lard (available in Latin markets)
2 cups masa harina
1 teaspoon baking powder
2 tablespoons pureed canned chipotle peppers
1 cup smoked chicken stock (standard stock will do)
salt

SMOKED CHICKEN FILLING:

1 medium yellow onion, diced
1 tablespoon unrefined corn oil
2 teaspoons minced garlic
2 cups smoked chicken, coarsely chopped
2 tablespoons pureed canned chipotle peppers (more to taste)
4 tablespoons chopped fresh chopped cilantro
salt

SMOKED CORN SALSA:

3 ears very fresh corn*
2 medium ripe tomatoes
1 small red onion
2 jalapeno peppers with seeds
1 sweet red pepper
2 teaspoons pureed canned chipotle peppers
juice of 2 limes
1/3 cup unrefined corn oil or extra-virgin olive oil
1/4 cup cilantro leaves

*good frozen corn can be substituted before fresh corn has come into season.

Soak the corn husks overnight in warm water. To prepare the tamale dough, beat the lard until light and fluffy. Add the masa harina, baking powder, pureed chipotle peppers, and a small amount of the stock. Mix the dough with your hands, adding more liquid if necessary until it can be formed into a ball. Taste the mixture and add salt if desired, though the smoked chicken stock may provide enough salt. Set the dough aside.

Saute the onions over medium heat until soft and transparent. Add the garlic and saute 2 minutes. Remove from the heat, add the chicken and chipotle peppers, toss together well. Taste the mixture and add more of the pureed peppers for a hotter mixture. Add the cilantro, toss again and add salt if necessary.

To make the salsa, remove the husks and silk from the corn and plunge the ears into a large pot of rapidly boiling water for 2 to 3 minutes. Remove and rinse in cool water. Cut the kernels from the cob and place them in a mixing bowl. Dice the tomatoes and add them to the corn. Dice the onion, remove the stems and seeds from the sweet pepper, cut it into small dice, and add it to the corn mixture. Stir in pureed chipotles, lime juice, corn or olive oil and clinatro leaves. Taste, adjust seasonings and chill until ready to use.

To assemble the tamales, dry the corn husks on tea towels. Lay a husk smooth side up. Place about 2 to 3 tablespoon of tamale dough in center of the husk, leaving at least 1/2 inch on either side and 2 inches on each end free of filling. Place a tablespoon or two of the chicken filling (see below) in center of tamale dough. Fold the husks over and overlap the edges, but not too tightly. Tie each end with a small piece of twine or a narrow strip of husk. Repeat the process until all of the dough and filling have been used.

Line a vegetable steamer with extra husks and stack the tamales seam side down, in the rack, no more than 3 layers high. Cover the tamales with corn husks, or if there are no more, a clean tea towel. Cover the pot and simmer over low heat for 50 minutes.

Let tamales rest 5 to 10 minutes before serving. Arrange on a large platter surrounding the bowl of corn salsa or place on individual serving plates, 2 to 3 per serving, with a healthy spoonful of corn salsa and a sprig of cilantro on the side.

Cold Mexican beer is the beverage of choice with these tamales, but any wine that can stand up to the heat of the pepper will work, too. Try a crisp Sauvignon Blanc, a fruity Gewurtztraminer.

Michele Anna Jordan, Owner
The Jaded Palate Catering Company

Michele Anna Jordon is also the author of a great new book for the visitor to Sonoma County, "A Cook's Tour of Sonoma," with resources, recipes, etc. RPH

Grilled Pesto-Stuffed Chicken Breasts

6 large boneless chicken breast
  halves with skin intact
olive oil
1/4 cup grated Asiago
3/4 cup grated jack cheese
1/4 cup coarsely chopped fresh
  basil

1 tablespoon aniseed, finely
  ground with mortar/pestle
salt and freshly ground pepper
1 tablespoon olive oil
3 tablespoons pine nuts
1 egg yolk
1/4 cup finely chopped sun-dried
  tomatoes

Combine Asiago, jack cheese, basil, 1 tablespoon olive oil, pine nuts and egg yolk in bowl of food processor until chopped fine, remove to bowl, stir in sun-dried tomatoes. (May prepare a day in advance.) Cover and refrigerate until stuffing is firm (30 minutes or more). Using fingers, gently form pocket (1-1/2 inch wide, 3 inch deep) between skin and meat entering from wider side of upper breast. Stuff filling in pocket (see below). Pat filling to uniform thickness. Press around opening with fingertips to enclose. Prepare barbecue grill (high heat). Brush chicken thoroughly with oil, sprinkle with ground aniseed, salt and pepper. Place skin side down on grill, cook 7 minutes. Turn over and cook until just springy to the touch, about 7 minutes or 170° internal temperature. Serve at once with roasted red pepper dressing.* Serves 6.

ROASTED RED PEPPER DRESSING:*

1 egg yolk
2 tablespoons Balsamic vinegar
1/2 cup sliced roasted red bell
  pepper
salt and freshly ground black pepper

1/4 tablespoon sun dried tomato
  paste or regular tomato paste
1/4 cup vegetable oil
1/4 cup walnut or hazelnut oil

Combine all ingredients except oils and salt and pepper in bowl of food processor. Process until smooth. Combine oils in measuring cup, pour slowly into processor while motor is running. Mix until slightly thickened. Season with salt and pepper.

You will enjoy our Blanc de Noirs with this!

Jamie Davies, Co-Owner
Schramsberg Vineyards & Cellars

Wild Duck Paté

2 wild ducks
1/2 pound of rabbit or chicken,
 if ducks are small
16 ounces bacon
2 large eggs, beaten
1 teaspoon salt
1 1/2 teaspoons freshly ground
 black pepper
4 tablespoons Brandy

8 large mushrooms, cut in half
 then sliced thickly
1/2 medium yellow onion, finely
 chopped
1 teaspoon chopped shallot
1/2 teaspoon freshly ground
 nutmeg
2 tablespoons vegetable oil
2 teaspoons butter

Slice duck breasts into finger length pieces and set aside. Remove all duck meat from bones. There should be approximately 2/3 pounds. Chicken or rabbit can supplement duck meat. Chop finely in food processor with 12 ounces of bacon, reserving 6 to 8 slices to line pan. Marinate mixture in bowl with eggs, salt, pepper and Brandy for 30 minutes. Meanwhile saute sliced mushrooms (reserving a few slices for decoration) shallot, onions and nutmeg in oil and butter until liquid is absorbed. Add to duck mixture when cool.

Line medium pate pan with bacon slices leaving some to fold over top of pate. Fill pan 1/3 with duck mixture, then lay strips of duck breasts. Repeat layering, finishing with duck mixture. Decorate top with sliced mushrooms and cover with bacon strips. Bake in 350° oven for 1 1/2 hours or until cooked through. Remove from oven, drain the fat and weigh down with foil and a weight such as can of food while cooling.

To serve, remove bacon on top and sides. Serve with French bread or crackers and a bottle of Wm. Wheeler R.S. Reserve - delicious for a picnic lunch by the pool or as an appetizer.

Ingrid Wheeler, Co-Owner
Wm. Wheeler Winery

Grilled Peking Duck Breast
with Shiitake Cabernet Sauce

8 full duck breasts, skinned
3 whole star anise
1 cup soy sauce
1 tablespoon minced ginger
1 tablespoon green onion

1 tablespoon honey
1 tablespoon minced orange peel
1 tablespoon minced garlic
1 tablespoon cilantro

Blend the above ingredients except for the duck breasts in a blender. Marinate for one hour before grilling.

SAUCE:

2 roast duck carcasses (from
  above)
1 pound fresh shiitake mushrooms
  (stems, pieces, etc.)
water

8 whole shiitake beveled
  (for garnish)
2 cups Cabernet
butter
drained & strained marinade
  (from above)

Cover duck carcasses with water. Add mushrooms and simmer for 2 to 3 hours. Strain stock and reserve the 8 whole mushrooms. Reduce stock to 6 cups. Add Cabernet and marinade and reduce to 2 cups. If necessary, thicken by whipping with pieces of butter. Grill duck breasts to medium (4 minutes per side). Slice and fan out on plate. Place reserved shiitake on top. Ladle sauce over.

Serve with Geyser Peak Reserve Cabernet.

Barbara Hom
Geyser Peak Winery

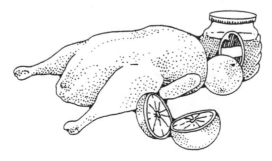

Caraway-Raspberry Chicken

6 chicken legs & thighs, boned
2 tablespoons vegetable oil
2 tablespoons flour
salt & pepper to taste
1/2 cup red raspberry vinegar

1/2 cup water
1 chicken bouillon cube
1/2 teaspoon caraway seeds
1/4 cup whipping cream
fresh raspberries for garnish

Flour chicken on both sides, sprinkle lightly with salt and pepper and brown in hot oil (skin side down first). When golden brown, remove from heat and drain oil and fat from pan. Return to heat. Add raspberry vinegar, water and bouillon cube. Sprinkle with caraway seeds. Cover and reduce heat to low simmer. Simmer for 40 minutes. Remove chicken to platter and place in warming oven. Reduce sauce to syrupy consistency. When ready to serve pour sauce over chicken and garnish. Serves 6.

We are indebted to Carmen Kozlowski for this recipe, which adds a whole new taste dimension to chicken!

Kozlowski Farms

Poulet Japonaise

1/4 cup melted margarine
1/4 cup Dijon mustard

2 cloves garlic

PANKO MIXTURE:

2 tablespoons grated Parmesan
  cheese
1 cup Panko Japanese
  breadcrumbs*

1 tablespoon minced parsley
6 boneless, skinless chicken
  breasts

DIJON SAUCE:

1/4 cup mayonnaise
1/4 cup yogurt

1/4 cup Dijon mustard
2 scallions, minced

Combine melted margarine with mustard and garlic and turn chicken breasts in this marinade, coating them completely. Dip and coat each breast in the panko mixture. Place in 8x13 inch rimmed baking pan, and bake in middle of preheated oven at 500° for 15 minutes. Cut crosswise into one inch slices, and arrange on plates, with a dollop of the sauce. Garnish the slices with thinly sliced whites from scallions.

*Available from Japanese section in foodmarkets.

Delightful served with rice and fresh asparagus, and paired with a light and dry Savignon Blanc.

Duane Bue

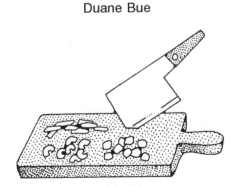

Chicken in Melon with Honeysuckle

4 cantaloupes
2 cups cooked chicken, diced
1 cup seedless grapes, peeled
1/2 cup mayonnaise

1 cup melon balls
3 tablespoons honeysuckle
  flowers
Honeysuckle sprigs to garnish

Halve the melons and discard the seeds. Scoop out flesh with a melon baller and set aside. Turn the empty melon halves upside down and leave to drain. Mix together the diced chicken, melon balls grapes and honeysuckle with the mayonnaise and pile the mixture into the drained melon shells. Chill well and top with a sprig of honeysuckle. Serves 8. This makes a stunning-looking dish for a summer buffet.

We suggest Bandiera Fume Blanc to accompany this dish.

Bandiera Winery

Chicken and Dried Tomatoes

4 chicken breast halves, skinless
  and boneless, each cut in 6 pieces
1 1/2 tablespoons butter
1 large shallot, diced (or 2
  tablespoons minced onion)
1 tablespoon Dijon mustard

2/3 cup heavy cream
2 tablespoons dry Vermouth or
  white wine
1-2 tablespoons dried tarragon
3 ounces dried tomato halves

Soften tomato halves using package directions and cut into narrow strips. Melt butter in skillet and saute chicken pieces for 4 to 5 minutes. Using a slotted spoon, remove chicken to platter. Add shallot, saute 1 minute, then add remaining ingredients to skillet. Simmer and stir until sauce thickens slightly. Return chicken to skillet and simmer until heated. Serve with pasta. Serves 5-6.

Waltenspiel's Kitchen
Timbercrest Farms

Chicken with Tomatoes and White Wine Sauce

5 boneless, skinless chicken breast halves
3 tablespoons butter
2 tablespoons olive oil
1 tablespoon chopped fresh rosemary
2 garlic cloves, crushed
salt & pepper to taste

2 tablespoons chopped shallots
1 14 ounce can plum Italian tomatoes
12 ounces fresh mushrooms, quartered
1/2 cup chicken broth
3/4 cup Chardonnay

Heat butter and oil in large skillet and brown flattened chicken breast. Season with salt, pepper and chopped rosemary. Remove chicken from skillet and keep warm. In remaining oil, saute garlic and shallots; add mushrooms and tomatoes and cook 5 minutes. Add chicken broth and wine; cook sauce for 10 minutes. When it has reduced, return chicken to the skillet and let it absorb the flavor for 3 minutes. Transfer chicken to warm plates and serve with tomato sauce. Preparation time: 30 minutes. Serves 5.

Chalk Hill Chardonnay goes well with this recipe.

Chalk Hill Winery

145

Chicken with Plums and Coriander

2 broiler chickens, about 2-1/2
  pounds each, cut in half
butter or margarine
1 1/2 cups fresh plums (4-6 plums
  depending on size)
salt & pepper

1 clove garlic, crushed
2 tablespoons chopped fresh
  coriander, or parsley
1/8 - 1/4 teaspoon red pepper
  sauce

Wash chickens and wipe dry. Brush well with butter or margarine.
Season with salt and pepper. Arrange skin side down on grill or broiler
rack. Chop plums and put into saucepan. Add garlic, coriander and red
pepper. Bring to a boil, then cook over medium heat until plums become
"saucy." This usually takes about 30-45 minutes. While sauce is cooking,
broil or grill chickens. During the last 15 minutes, baste the chickens with
plum sauce. Serve the chicken garnished with more sauce and fresh
coriander. Serves 4.

This is a great early summer barbecue dish when plums are fresh from
the trees. I like to add about 1/4 cup Sea Ridge Pinot Noir to sauce to
help marry it to the final dish.

Serve Sea Ridge Pinot Noir.

                Dee Wickham
                Sea Ridge Winery

Chicken Charmoula

6 half chicken breasts, skinned and boned
1 clove garlic (about 1 teaspoon) minced
2 tablespoons Italian (flat leaf) parsley, chopped
2 tablespoons cilantro, chopped
1 teaspoon salt
3 teaspoons ground cumin
3 teaspoons sweet paprika
1/2 teaspoon Cayenne pepper
4 tablespoons lemon juice
4 tablespoons olive oil
1 cup homemade or good commercial mayonnaise*
cilantro sprigs for garnish

This recipe was inspired by a traditional Moroccan seasoning. Arrange chicken in a glass or ceramic dish. Mince garlic in food processor fitted with steel blade. Add all remaining herbs and spices and process. Add lemon juice and olive oil and puree. Spread half the spice mixture over all surfaces of chicken. Cover and marinate, refrigerated, 2 to 12 hours. Refrigerate balance of spice mixture.

Prepared fire in grill or heat broiler. Grill or broil chicken about 3 minutes per side. Meanwhile, mix reserved spice mixture with the mayonnaise to make sauce.

Serve each piece of chicken with a dollop of sauce, garnished with cilantro sprigs. This dish is equally enjoyable served hot or at room temperature. Serves 4 to 6.

*The diet conscious will find a squeeze of lemon a very satisfying substitute for the mayonnaise sauce.

Mary Evely, Chef
Simi Winery

Heriseh

1 small chicken	paprika
1 1/2 cups whole wheat zezads*	4 cups chicken broth
5 cups water	salt & white pepper to taste
1/2 cube butter	

Place water and chicken broth in large pot. Bring to a boil. Clean chicken and place in pot. Cook until chicken falls apart. Cool. Remove bones and skin. Add zezads* and salt. Cook until water is absorbed. (It is best to cook it, covered, in a 325° oven.) Stir every hour until it looks like mush. Chicken should be completely blended. Taste for salt and pepper. Beat a couple of times real hard and fast. Serve in bowls with melted butter and paprika on top. Cumin is also used as a garnish.

For a Heriseh less rich and easier to make, use 4 cups chicken or turkey without skin, such as canned chicken or turkey.

*These zezads may be purchased in Armenian or similar grocery stores. Indian grocers may have them under the name of Gorgords. Or, use large size pearl barley.

Ayn Ryan Coleman, Co-Owner
Adler Fels Winery

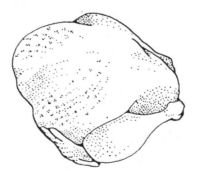

Rolled Turkey Breast with Fruit Sauce

1 turkey breast, approximately 3 pounds, butterflied
1/4 cup dried apricots, chopped
1/4 cup cranberry relish
salt and pepper to taste

Butterfly the turkey breast, season with salt and pepper. Spread dried fruit and cranberry relish over surface of butterflied turkey breast. Roll up like a roast and tie. Roast in 450° oven for approximately 40-45 minutes. Serves 10 people.

SAUCE:

1/4 cup sugar
1/2 cup raspberry vinegar
1/2 cup Riesling

1 cup orange juice
2 cups turkey stock

To make sauce: Caramelize sugar in pot. Add vinegar, orange juice and wine. Reduce to thick and syrupy consistency. Add turkey stock, bring to boil and reduce until consistency of sauce. Should yield 2 cups of sauce.

Accompany this entree with a chilled bottle of Jekel Johannisburg Riesling.

Donna Wegener
Chef de Cuisine, Jekel Vineyards

Chardonnay Chicken Marinade

2 cups Chardonnay
2 sprigs Rosemary, broken up
3/4 cup oil
4 large garlic cloves, cut coarsely
1 tablespoon Worcestershire sauce
paprika.

1/4 cup ketchup
1/4 cup barbecue sauce, any
  brand
salt, pepper
Italian seasonings

Pour over chicken. For best results, let stand for several hours or even overnight.

Serve with a Chardonnay or a White Zinfandel from Sausal.

Roselee Demostene & Cindy Martin, Co-Owners
Sausal Winery

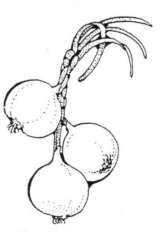

Chicken Breast with Apricot

toothpicks
1 tablespoon clarified butter
2 chicken breasts, boned, skinned
  and lightly pounded
1/2 cup dried apricots
1/2 cup Brut Champagne
2 teaspoons sugar

2 cups spinach leaves, washed
salt, white pepper
1 tablespoon cornstarch, mixed
  with 1 teaspoon cold water
1 tablespoon apricot jam
1/2 teaspoon soy sauce

Steam spinach in a little water with salt, pepper and dash of nutmeg. Drain well. In a saucepan, heat champagne, apricots, and sugar to a boil. Reduce heat to medium and cook for 5 minutes. Remove apricots from liquid; add soy sauce and apricot jam to Champagne. Thicken for a glaze by adding cornstarch mixture. Bring to a boil and turn heat off.

Lay chicken breast skin side down and place a thin layer, approximately 1-2 leaves thick, of spinach on the chicken breast. Place cooked apricots on center of breasts. Roll breast up and secure middle and ends with toothpicks. Sprinkle lightly with salt and white pepper. In a saute pan, heat clarified butter on medium high heat. Add chicken breasts and saute until golden on all sides (approximately 5 minutes). Turn heat to low, cover and cook for eight more minutes.

Pour in glaze, mixing well. Remove toothpicks and slice chicken breast 1/2 to 3/4 inch thick. Serve warm or cold. Serves 2.

Serve with Korbel Brut Champagne

F. Korbel & Bros., Inc.

VEGETABLES

Sweet Corn Pie

8 ears of corn
1 cup of milk
1 tablespoon butter
1 tablespoon flour
4 egg whites
20 black olives
1/2 cup raisins

1 hard boiled egg, cut in wedges
4 egg yolks
1 teaspoon confectioners sugar
1 1/2 pounds ground beef
1 large onion, chopped
cumin, oregano, salt, pepper

Saute onion until transparent, add the meat and saute until cooked; add raisins, the hard boiled egg, salt, pepper, oregano, cumin and olives. This preparation is called "Pino." If you like your food spicy, add a few drops of chili sauce or serve with picante sauce. Grind the corn kernels. Cook with the butter, flour and milk in a heavy pan, stirring continuously. Remove from heat. Beat the egg yolks and add to the corn mixture. Whip the egg whites until they are stiff and fold into corn mixture. Arrange the "Pino" in a baking dish or in individual ramekins and cover it with the corn mixture. Spread a little sugar on top and bake in 350° oven until golden. Serves 6.

Clos Du Val winemaker, Bernard Portet, says "I am a beast in the kitchen, and learned my love and appreciation of fine food from my mother, my wife and other fine chefs." This delicious Chilean dish comes from his wife, Helia. It is delightful as a main course at dinner or for a luncheon. Serve piping hot from the oven with a mixed green salad or a tomato, onion and cilantro salad - very Chilean! Enjoy a glass of Clos Du Val Chardonnay or Pinot Noir with this wonderful sweet corn pie!

Mrs. Bernard Portet
Clos Du Val Winery

Herbed Shallots in Phyllo

1 package phyllo
36 medium to large shallots
3 tablespoons olive oil

1 tablespoon butter
1/4 cup melted butter for phyllo
Fresh chopped herbs (basil,
   thyme, marjoram, chervil,
   or tarragon or dry herbs mixed)

Preheat oven to 400°. In a heavy skillet combine butter and oil. Add shallots and saute for about 2 minutes, stirring so they do not burn. Turn heat to lowest setting and let shallots cook to a richly glazed brown, about 10 to 20 minutes. Remove from heat. Cut 5 inch squares of phyllo. Keep remaining phyllo covered. You will need 24 squares. Brush phyllo square with melted butter. Make two layers of phyllo. Place 3 shallots in center of phyllo square. Sprinkle liberally with herbs. Draw up corners and pinch together. Bake packets until golden brown, about 4 to 5 minutes. Serves 4 to 6.

Serve with Schramsberg Reserve.

Jamie Davies, Co-Owner
Schramsberg Vineyard & Cellars

Corn Pudding

6 ears of corn, grated
6 tablespoons butter
1/2 teaspoon baking powder
3 eggs, separated

1 teaspoon salt
1 teaspoon sugar
1 cup milk
1/2 green pepper, minced fine
1 teaspoon flour

Cream butter well, add beaten yolks of eggs, grated corn and other ingredients; add the egg whites beaten stiff last. Bake in slow oven at 325° for 30 minutes or until set so that the pudding does not adhere to a knife or spoon insert to test.

This is a very old wine country recipe that is still a favorite in some of our local restaurants.

Tomato Tarts with Pancetta, Mushrooms Basil and Gruyere Cheese

8 cups chopped tomatoes (skin and seeds removed)
4 ounces pancetta (may substitute bacon), cut into strips
1 tablespoon olive oil
1 chopped onion
1/2 cup Sauvignon Blanc
2 cloves garlic, finely minced
1 cup fresh chicken stock, reduced to 1/4 cup

2 teaspoons sugar
1 cup sliced mushrooms
4 tablespoons butter
4 ounces prosciutto or ham, cut into strips
salt & pepper
1 tablespoon chopped fresh basil
1 cup grated Gruyere cheese

Place tomatoes into a large saucepan and bring to a simmer. While tomatoes come to a simmer, saute bacon in olive oil until slightly crisp. Add onion and continue cooking until lightly browned. To the simmering tomatoes, add the Sauvignon Blanc, garlic, chicken stock, sugar. Saute the sliced mushrooms in butter and add to the tomato sauce along with the sauteed bacon and onion. Add the proscuitto, basil and salt and pepper to taste. Simmer filling until it is thick. Sprinkle tart shells (see below) with grated Gruyere cheese. Fill with tomato filling and sprinkle top with more cheese. Heat in a 350° oven and serve immediately.

PATE BRISSE:

2 cups unsifted flour
1 1/2 sticks butter

1 teaspoon salt
1/3 to 1/2 cup cold water

On a table place the flour, butter, and salt. Cut into large crumbs. Make a well in the center and add the water. Bring flour in from sides and gently mix. With the heel of your hand press out dough into long strokes, one stroke at a time. Gently gather into a mound and chill 2 hours. Roll chilled dough to about 1/4" thick and cut it to fit individual tart tins. Fit pastry into tins and press firmly against the bottom and sides. Prick with fork and chill again approximately 1 hour. Fit pastry with paper or foil and fill with beans or rice. Bake in preheated 400° oven for 12-15 minutes. Remove paper, and if necessary, continue baking shells until light brown. Wine: Chateau Souverain Sauvignon Blanc.

Patricia Windisch, Executive Chef/General Manager
Chateau Souverain Restaurant

Caponata
(an Italian Vegetable Medley)

1 eggplant, about 1 pound
2 large green peppers
2 onions, 6 ounces each
1/2 pound fresh plum tomatoes
4 tablespoons olive oil
3/4 cup chopped fresh Italian
  parsley

2 garlic cloves, peeled
2 tablespoons red wine vinegar
4 tablespoons capers
1/3 teaspoon Italian seasoning
salt & pepper

Wash and trim the eggplant, do not peel. Cut eggplant into cubes. there will be about 2 cups. Soak cubes in cold water with 1 tablespoon salt for each quart of water. Soak for 10 minutes. Drain and pat dry. While eggplant is soaking; wash and trim the peppers, remove ribs and seeds and chop. Peel and chop onion. Wash tomatoes, remove hard part near the stem and chop; should be 1 cup.

Heat the olive oil and add chopped or pressed garlic into the oil. Add onion and saute until translucent. Add peppers and eggplant and saute, stirring often, 5 minutes. Add vinegar, capers, Italian seasoning and cook for 2 to 3 minutes. Add tomatoes and cook for 5 minutes longer. Salt and pepper to taste. Add parsley. Serve warm or cold. Makes 5 to 6 cups. Serves 8.

Magliulo's Restaurant & Pensione

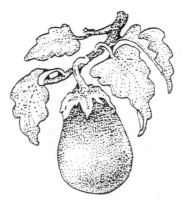

Zucchini and Carrots

2 1/2 cups carrots
2 1/2 cups zucchini
2 tablespoons olive oil

1 clove garlic, crunched
1 tablespoon lemon juice
3 tablespoons Sweet Vermouth

Cut the vegetables in julienne style. Use a large frying pan or wok, add oil to *hot* pan. Saute garlic and carrots for 2 minutes and then add zucchini. Toss about 2 minutes. Add lemon juice and wine. Toss about briefly, remove from heat and serve.

Jeani Martini
Martini & Pratti Wines

Broccoli Casserole

3 cups cooked short grain
  brown rice
1 pound mushrooms sliced or
  quartered, sauteed
1 large onion chopped and
  sauteed with 3 cloves
  minced garlic

2 1/2 cups shredded Jack cheese
2 cups basic white sauce
splash of white wine
salt & pepper
basil
1 large bunch broccoli (about
  3 cups) broken into flowerettes
  (peel and chop stems) parboiled
  and drained (or cauliflower)

Combine all ingredients and pour into baking dish. Top with toasted cashew pieces or sunflower seed if desired. Bake covered for 30 minutes in preheated oven at 350°. Uncover and bake 10 minutes more to a golden brown.

The Sonoma Cheese Factory

As served at the Sonoma Valley Vintners' Picnic in the Park.

Charmian London's Baked Beans

1 pound small Great Northern
  or Navy beans
24 ounces dark beer
1 pint water
1 pint strong coffee
1 medium onion, chopped
1 tablespoon ginger, chopped fine
2 ounces maple syrup

4 ounces black strap molasses
1/2 cup brown sugar
2 teaspoons mustard powder
1/2 teaspoon black pepper
1 large onion stuck with 4 cloves
6 ounces diced salt pork
1 pound duck meat
1 tablespoon wild thyme

Soak beans overnight in beer. Mix the coffee, 1 cup water, maple syrup, molasses 1/4 cup brown sugar and the mustard powder into the beans. Place in a covered casserole; add the large onion with the cloves and the diced salt pork. Bring to a simmer on top of the stove. Cover and place in preheated oven 300° for 2 hours.

Meanwhile, cut the duck into pieces, pepper it and brown it in duck fat adding the onion and ginger. Pour off excess fat and add 1 cup of water to deglaze the pan. Now add the duck, onion, ginger and liquid from the pan to the casserole of beans. Add the thyme, cover tightly; return to oven for 2 1/2 hours more.

Check often to make sure the beans are covered with liquid; add water if needed. After 2 1/2 hours, remove the lid and sprinkle the top of the beans with remaining 1/4 cup of brown sugar, return to the oven for 1/2 hour and serve.

The Wild Thyme Food Library

Courtesy Sonoma Valley Cuisine Society

This is really a meal unto itself, with its duck meat and salt pork, but we hid it in among the vegetables so you could discover it for yourself.

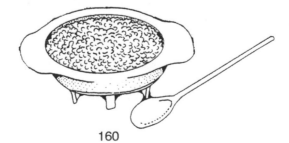

Rosemary-Blue Cheese Potatoes

3 pounds red potatoes, cubed
4 tablespoons blue cheese
2 teaspoons minced fresh
 Rosemary
dash of Hungarian paprika or
 Cayenne

3 to 4 tablespoons olive oil
4 tablespoons minced fresh
 parsley
dash of salt & pepper

Cook the potatoes 10 minutes in a pot of rapidly boiling water. Drain. toss potatoes with olive oil, rosemary, parsley and salt. Place potatoes on an ungreased baking sheet. Sprinkle Hungarian paprika or Cayenne and crumbled blue cheese on potatoes. Place potatoes in oven on top rack and broil until lightly browned. Remove and serve.

Serve with Bouchaine Pinot Noir for 10-12 guests.

Bouchaine Vineyards

Ratatouille

1 small eggplant, cut into
 1/8" dices
1 teaspoon salt
1/4 cup olive oil
2 cloves minced garlic
2 teaspoons chopped shallots
1 red pepper, cut into 1/8"
 dices

2 plum or Roma tomatoes,
 peeled, seeded and diced
1 teaspoon fresh thyme
1/2 teaspoon fresh oregano
1 teaspoon chopped fresh basil
1 tablespoon Sherry wine vinegar
salt & pepper to taste
1 medium zucchini, cut into
 1/8" dices

Toss eggplant with salt and let stand for 10 minutes. Drain and pat dry. Heat oil in a skillet and saute garlic and shallots. Add red pepper and eggplant and cook for 2 minutes. Add zucchini, tomatoes, and herbs and cook for one minute more. Add vinegar, salt and pepper, stir well, then remove from heat. Serve warm or at room temperature. Nice to serve in a hollow tomato. Serves 6.

Bettina Dreyer, Vice President
Grand Cru Vineyards

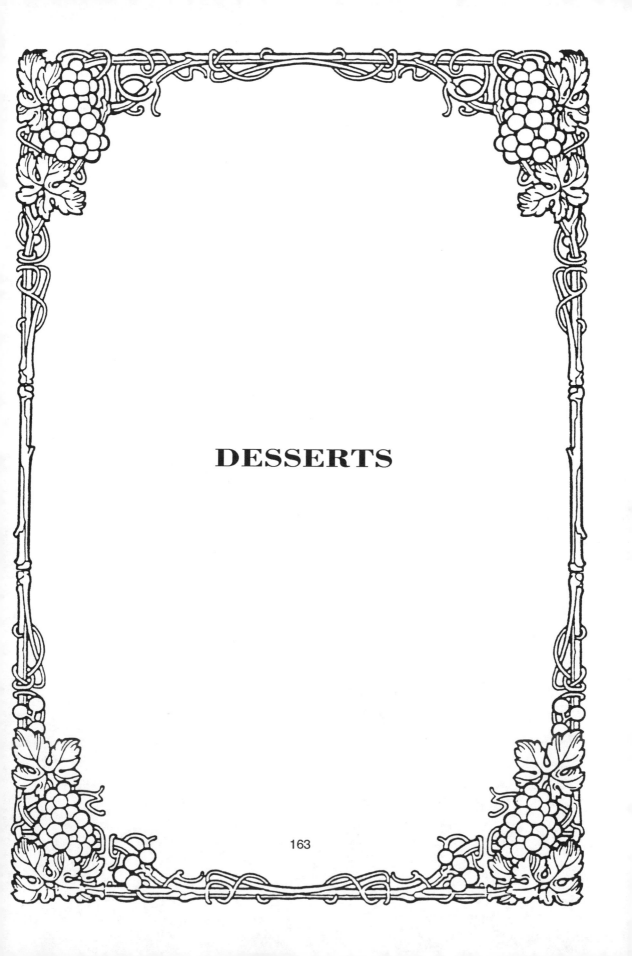

DESSERTS

Raspberry Amaretto Custard Tarts

2 cups milk
3/4 cup sugar
1/2 cup four
1/8 teaspoon salt
raspberries
crust (see below)

2 beaten egg yolks
5 tablespoons butter
1 teaspoon vanilla
1/4 cup Amaretto
1 jar Apricot jam, melted
  and put through a sieve
  (may need to thin)

Scald milk. Mix the sugar, flour and salt. Add to hot milk and cook until thick. Add beaten egg yolks and continue cooking approximately 3 minutes, beating constantly. Stir in butter, vanilla and Amaretto. May thin with cream. Stir to cool. Put a small layer of custard in the bottom of each tart shell. Fill with raspberries and glaze with melted jam.

CRUST:

1 cup flour
1/3 teaspoon salt
2 tablespoons sugar

6 tablespoons butter
3 tablespoons ice water

Preheat oven to 425°. Place flour, salt and sugar on a table and mix well. Cut in the butter using your fingertips making coarse crumbs. Make a well in the center of the mixture and add the water. Bring flour in from sides and very gently mix. With the heel of hand, press out dough, one stroke at a time. Gently gather into a mound and chill 2 hours. Roll out dough and cut to fit individual tart tins. Fit pastry into tins and press firmly against the bottom and sides. Prick with a fork. Chill. Fit pastry with foil and fill in with beans or rice. Bake 12 to 15 minutes, remove foil and beans and continue baking if necessary to a light golden color.

Patricia Windisch, Manager
Chateau Souverain Restaurant

Mint Crepes with Mangoes in Ginger Syrup

2 large ripe mangoes
2 inch piece of fresh ginger
  Julienne cut
2 cups water
4 tablespoons sugar

1 tablespoon crystallized
  ginger
2 tablespoons lime juice
zest of 1 lime
mint sprays for garnish

Peel and dice mangoes and add fresh ginger, chill. In saucepan, mix water, sugar, zest of lime and crystallized ginger, bring to boil. Reduce heat and simmer until liquid is reduced by half. Leave to cool. Add lime juice and pour over mangoes. Roll crepes (see below) into cones and fill each crepe with 3 tablespoons of filling. Decorate with a sprig of mint.

CREPES:

1 cup flour
pinch of salt
2 eggs
1 teaspoon sugar

1 1/4 cup milk
1 tablespoon butter
1/2 cup Julienne mint leaves

Put all ingredients except butter and mint leaves into food processor. Blend until smooth. Stir in mint leaves. Chill for one hour. Melt butter in crepe pan. When sizzling, pour in a small amount of batter so that the pan is covered thinly and evenly. Cook for one minute over high heat, flip and cook another 30 seconds.

Serve with Matanzas Creek Sauvignon Blanc.

Christina May Evans, Chef
Matanzas Creek Winery

Polenta Pudding with
Fresh Blackberry Compote and
"Petite Liqueur," Mascarpone Whipped Cream

1 cup polenta
2 cups bread flour
2 egg yolks
4 eggs

BERRY COMPOTE:

4 cups fresh blackberries
1/2 cup granulated sugar
1/4 cup "Petite Liqueur"

1/4 Tahitian vanilla bean (scrape
  inside)
5 cups powdered sugar
1 1/2 cup sweet butter

MASCARPONE CREAM:

4 ounces mascarpone
8 ounces whipping cream
1 1/2 ounces sugar
*all whipped to a soft peak

In an electric mixer beat the soft butter, sugar and vanilla until creamy. Beat in the eggs and egg yolks one at a time. Fold in flour and polenta. Pour into 12" greased and floured cake pan. Bake 1 hour, 15 minutes in a preheated oven at 325°. Unmold on a rack and let cool. Place cake in a larger size cake pan. Pour cooked berries and juices on top and around cake, cover and soak overnight. Cut cake into slices and garnish with mascarpone cream on top and a few fresh blackberries. Add a few drops of "Petite Liqueur," a mint tip and some of the berry juices around the cake. Serve at room temperature.

This elegant dessert marries well with Chandon Blanc de Noirs.

Philippe Jeanty,
Chef de Cuisine, Domaine Chandon

Red Raspberry Crepes

1 4 ounce container whipped
  cream cheese
10 dessert crepes (see recipe)
3 tablespoons sugar
1 cup raspberry cider
1 tablespoon butter or margarine
1 pint fresh raspberries or one
  10 ounce package frozen,
  thawed and drained

2 tablespoons toasted slivered
  almonds
1 teaspoon cornstarch
1 teaspoon orange liqueur
1/4 cup toasted slivered almonds
1 tablespoon lemon juice

Spread cheese over uncrowned side of each dessert crepe, leaving 1/4 inch rim around edge. Sprinkle each crepe with a portion of the 2 tablespoon of almonds. Fold each crepe into a triangle by folding in half, then half again. Cover crepes, set aside. In a 10 inch skillet combine the sugar, cornstarch, and dash salt. Stir in apple raspberry cider and butter or margarine. Cook and stir 2 minutes more. Stir in liqueur, lemon juice and barriers. Add crepes to sauce; heat through. Sprinkle the 1/4 cup almonds a top. Serve immediately. Serves 10.

CREPES:

1 cup flour
2 tablespoons sugar
1/8 teaspoon salt

2 eggs
1 1/2 cups milk
1/4 cup butter, melted

Beat with rotary beater until well mixed. Heat lightly greased 6 inch skillet, remove from heat, spoon in 2 tablespoons of batter, lift and tilt skillet to spread thinly, return to heat, do not turn over. Invert pan over paper towel to remove crepe. Repeat for other crepes. Makes 16.

Carol Kozlowski-Every
Kozlowski Farms

168

Orange Custard with
Strawberries and Muscat Canelli

2 cups milk
slivered zest of 2 oranges
2 eggs
4 egg yolks
1/2 cup sugar

1 teaspoon vanilla
2 cups strawberries, cut in half
1 375ml Muscat Canelli
6 custard cups

Preheat oven to 350°. Scald milk with the orange zest. In large mixing bowl, beat the eggs and lightly stir in the sugar. Add the milk slowly, stirring constantly. Add the vanilla and blend well. Strain and pour into the cups. Place the cups in a shallow baking pan. Fill the pan with boiling water to 1/2 way up the sides of the cups. Bake in center of oven for about 35 minutes until the custard feels firm when pressed.

Remove from water, cool and chill in refrigerator for at least 2 hours. Meanwhile, put Muscat in small saucepan, bring to a boil and reduce to 1/4 cup or syrup consistency and chill. Toss with strawberries 1/2 hour before serving. Unmold custard onto individual plates.

Surround with strawberries and drizzle with the syrup that remains form the strawberries. Serve immediately. Serves 6.

You'll enjoy our Muscat Canelli with this.

Stella Fleming, Executive Chef
Glen Ellen Winery

Bittersweet Chocolate Souffle

8 ounces bittersweet chocolate,
  in small chunks
1/3 cup strong coffee
2 tablespoons sweet butter
2 tablespoons flour
1 cup milk
3 egg yolks
1 teaspoon vanilla extract

4 egg whites
1/8 teaspoon cream of tartar
1/4 cup sugar
Garnish:
2 tablespoons powdered sugar
2/3 cup heavy cream
1 tablespoon Grand Marnier
1 tablespoon sugar

Butter 8 6-ounce souffle cups. Sprinkle with granulated sugar. Melt chocolate with coffee in double boiler over barely simmering water (or 2 minutes on high in microwave). Stir until smooth. Melt butter in a small saucepan. Add flour and cook briefly. Add milk gradually, whisking continuously until you have a smooth sauce. Continue whisking over medium heat until sauce thickens.

Remove from heat and let cool slightly. Add chocolate and whisk smooth. Mix in egg yolks and vanilla. Beat egg whites with cream of tartar until soft peaks form. Add sugar gradually, beating until whites are stiff but not dry. Fold 1/3 of whites into chocolate mixture to lighten it, then fold in remaining whites. Divide mixture, among the 8 prepared cups, place on a baking sheet and bake on the lower shelf of a 375° oven for about 17 minutes.

Whip cream with Grand Marnier and granulated sugar. Remove souffles from oven, dust with powdered sugar and serve immediately with the whipped cream. Serves 8.

Mary Evely, Chef
Simi Winery

Port Chocolate with Chocolate

2 ounces (2 squares) unsweetened baking chocolate
1 cup sugar
2 large eggs
1/2 teaspoon vanilla

1/4 teaspoon salt
1/2 cup sifted all-purpose flour
1/2 cup chopped walnuts (op)
Port chocolate sauce (see below)
1/2 cup unsalted butter

Coarsely chop chocolate squares. Heat butter in a heavy saucepan over medium-low heat until half melted. Add chocolate and stir with a wooden spoon until chocolate and butter are melted and blended. Remove from heat. Stir in sugar, stirring until dissolved. Add eggs, one at a time, and beat with a spoon after each addition until mixture is thoroughly combined and shiny. Stir in vanilla and salt. Stir in flour.

Turn into buttered 9-inch round layer cake pan and spread smooth. Bake in a 350° oven until slightly firm to touch and toothpick inserted in center shows mixture is a little moist, about 25 minutes. Let cool in pan on a rack. To serve: cut into wedges and top each with warm sauce. Serves 12. Note: if you want less consistency of pure chocolate, add 1/2 cup chopped walnuts to base batter before baking.

PORT CHOCOLATE SAUCE:

1 package (4 ounces) sweet baking chocolate

1/2 cup Port

Combine in top part of double boiler over hot (not boiling) water the chocolate, coarsely chopped and the Port. Heat and whisk until smooth. Makes about 1 cup, or topping for 6 to 8 dessert servings.

Shirley Sarvis, Consulting Chef
Ficklin Vineyards

Shirley Sarvis, who has written more than a dozen cookbooks, created this recipe for Ficklin Vineyards Port Wine. It is a delicious exotic dessert, with intense chocolate flavors in harmony with the spirit and vibrancy of Port wine.

Port Torte

3 large egg whites
1/4 teaspoon cream of tartar
1 cup sugar
1 teaspoon vanilla
1/8 teaspoon salt

1 cup graham cracker crumbs
1 cup chopped walnuts
1/2 cup Port
1 1/2 pints vanilla ice cream
1 tablespoon finely grated semi-
sweet baking chocolate

In a large bowl, beat egg whites with cream of tartar until frothy. Beat in sugar, 2 tablespoons at a time, beating well after each addition; beat until mixture is stiff and glossy. Beat in vanilla and salt. Gently fold in crumbs and nuts. Spread evenly in buttered 9 inch pie pan. Bake in 350° oven for 25 minutes. Cool on a rack. To serve, cut torte into wedges, and place each on a slightly scooped dessert plate; drizzle each with Port, then top with ice cream and a sprinkling of chocolate. Serves 8.

Shirley Sarvis, Consulting Chef
Ficklin Vineyards

Shirley Sarvis loves to mate Port wine and chocolate. This torte is proof of a happy marriage.

Chocolate Chestnut Truffles

16 ounces chocolate (semi-sweet
  or bittersweet)
2 cups heavy cream
1/2 cup sweet butter

6 tablespoons sugar
5 tablespoons Amaretto
1/2 cup chestnut puree
  (unsweetened)

Melt chocolate. In another pot, melt cream, butter and sugar. Add cream mixture to chocolate. Stir in Amaretto. Add chestnut puree (be sure chocolate mixture is not too hot). Chill in refrigerator until firm enough to work with and then roll into balls. Chill. Makes approximately 45 truffles.

Serve with Lyeth Alexander Valley Red Wine.

Donna Wegener, Chef de Cuisine
Lyeth Vineyards

Strawberry Extravaganza

1 1/2 cups all purpose flour
1/2 cup butter
1/2 cup crushed almonds
1 egg
2 8 ounce packages cream cheese,
  softened

2 cups powdered sugar
1 teaspoon grated orange peel
1 quart fresh strawberries,
  cleaned and halved
1 cup strawberry jam

Heat oven to 400°. Place steel blade into food processor. Add first 3 ingredients. Turn on and add egg through chute. Process just until ball forms. Roll out to 12 inch circle. Place onto pizza pan. Prick with fork. Bake 10-12 minutes, cool. Beat cream cheese, sugar and orange peel until smooth. Spread over crust. Arrange strawberries on filling. Stir jam until smooth, spoon over berries. Chill thoroughly. Decorate with sweetened whipped cream and garnish with toasted slivered almonds. Serves 12.

Kozlowski Farms

Mousse au Chocolate

5 large eggs, separated
scant 1/2 pound premium quality
  semisweet chocolate, broken
  into small pieces
1 teaspoon unsalted butter

Beat yolks until thick and light colored. In top of double boiler over hot (not boiling) water, melt chocolate and butter. Stir until smooth. Gradually beat warm chocolate into yolks. With clean beaters in a separate bowl, beat whites until nearly stiff but not dry. Immediately, thoroughly fold one third of the whites into chocolate mixture to lighten it. Gently fold in remaining whites. Turn into a pretty crystal serving bowl, about 1 1/2 quart capacity (or turn into individual small dessert pots). Cover and chill until set, about 3 hours. Serves 6-8.

Recommended with, or just after, our 1986 Napa Valley Cabernet Sauvignon.

Mrs. Mitsuko Shrem
Clos Pegase Winery

Caramel Nut Torte

2 1/4 cup flour
1/2 cup sugar
pinch of salt
7 ounces butter, softened

1 egg
1 yolk (reserve white)
1 teaspoon vanilla

Cream butter until it becomes smooth and pale. Add sugar and mix well. Add egg and yolk one at a time, beating well after each addition. Add vanilla. Mix salt and flour together then add to butter mixture mixing just until flour is well distributed. Remove from bowl and form into a ball. Wrap in plastic and refrigerate until firm, about one hour. Roll out the dough for the crust and line pan. Carefully spread almond cream (see below) on bottom of crust. Pre-bake in a 350° oven until lightly golden brown, about 10 minutes. Makes two 8x2 inch spring form pans. Place nut mixture (see below) into prebaked shells and arrange a lattice dressing on top with extra dough. Bake at 375° for 1/2 hour. Cool completely before serving.

ALMOND CREAM FILLING:

1 cup sliced natural almonds
1/4 cup sugar
2 tablespoons butter, softened

1 egg white
1 tablespoon flour

In a food processor or blender pulverize the almonds and sugar together. Add the butter and egg white and blend well. Remove from blender and stir in flour by hand. Mixture should be a creamy paste.

CARAMEL NUT FILLING:

1 1/4 cup sugar
1 cup heavy cream

3 cups whole nuts (mix of
    walnuts, almonds, hazelnuts,
    pecans, cashews, pistachios

Lightly toast nuts in a 400° oven, let cool and rub between hands to remove any loose skins. Place 1/4 cup of the sugar in a medium size heavy bottom pan and set on medium high heat. Move sugar around until it liquifies and begins to caramelize. Add remaining sugar 1/4 cup at a time stirring after each addition until mixture becomes liquid again. Remove pan from heat after last addition and slowly pour cream into sugar, stirring constantly. Return to low heat if mixture stiffens up. Add nuts to caramel and stir to mix well.

Beverly Salinger, Resident Chef
Frogs Leap Winery

This 3-step recipe is very unusual and very delicious. Well worth the effort.

Torta Di Noce (Walnut Torte)

3 egg whites
1 cup sugar
1 teaspoon vanilla
1 cup walnuts, shelled

1 cup graham crackers
4 ounces chocolate chips
2 tablespoons sour cream

Beat egg whites until stiff. Gradually add the sugar until mixture is very stiff. Fold in vanilla. Pass walnuts through food processor. Pass graham crackers through food processor. Fold in the walnuts and graham crackers. Spread in an ungreased 9 inch springform pan. Bank 20-30 minutes at 350°. Cool. Melt chocolate chips. Add the sour cream. Spread chocolate frosting on cooled torte. Serves 8.

Serve with Geyser Peak Late Harvest Riesling.

Anne Vercelli
Geyser Peak Winery

Apricot Crown

1 cup dried apricots	1 teaspoon lemon juice
1/2 cup sugar	1/2 cup chopped toasted
1 large egg	blanched almonds
1/4 teaspoon grated lemon rind	2 pounds puff pastry
	1 egg, lightly beaten

Put apricots in a saucepan with water to cover. Cook over low heat until soft. Drain and puree. Add remaining filling ingredients except nuts. Cool. Divide puff pastry in half. Roll, then cut a circle 10" in diameter 1/4" thick and place on parchment lined baking sheet. Roll and cut a circle 11" in diameter 1/4" thick.

Sprinkle nuts; mound filling in center 11" in diameter 1/4" thick. Sprinkle nuts; mound filling in center of 10" circle, leaving a 1-1/2" border. Moisten outside edge of base with water. Cover with 11" circle. Make a scalloped border by pressing the outside edge of a knife at 2" intervals. Cut a small circle in center of pastry. Cut small curving lines from center to circle to outside scallop. Chill 1 hour. Glaze with egg. Bake in preheated 425° oven 30 minutes. Reduce heat to 375°. Bake for 20 minutes or until golden brown. Serves 10-12.

Serve while still warm with Freemark Abbey's Edelwein Gold.

Sandra Learned, Consulting Chef
Freemark Abbey Vineyard

Apple Trifle

pound cake
cinnamon apple jelly
1 cup apple cider
1/4 cup Brandy

1 cup applesauce
vanilla custard
whipped cream
finely chopped walnuts

In a large glass bowl, arrange slices of pound cake that have been spread with cinnamon apple jelly and put together like sandwiches. Mix 1 cup apple cider and 1/4 cup Brandy and pour slowly over cake slices so all is absorbed. Spoon a cup or so of apple sauce over this and on top of the apple sauce pour a batch of vanilla custard. (You may either make your own from scratch or use instant pudding mix.) At serving time cover the chilled conglomeration with whipped cream, sprinkled with finely chopped walnuts. Serve with a big spoon into individual fruit dishes, being sure to get some of everything for everybody!

Helen Caswell, Owner
Caswell Winter Creek Farm and Vineyards

Late Harvest Pears

4 large pears, peeled, halved
  and cored
1 cup water
thin slices of preserved ginger

2 tablespoons sugar
1/2 teaspoon vanilla
1/4 cup Gewurztraminer
whipped cream

In a shallow pan arrange the pears flat side down. In one cup of water dissolve 2 tablespoons sugar and 1/2 teaspoon vanilla. Pour over pears. cover tightly and cook slowly until tender but firm. Add small amount of water and chill. Arrange in small fruit dishes, allowing 2 halves per serving, and pour on about 1/4 cup of Gewurztraminer. Top with a dollop of sweetened whipped cream flavored with a few drops of vanilla and garnished with thin slices of preserved ginger.

Helen Caswell, Owner
Caswell Winter Creek Farm and Vineyards

Quick and Easy Wine Cake

1 package yellow cake mix
1 4 1/2 ounce package instant
  vanilla pudding
4 eggs

3/4 cup oil
3/4 cup Grey Reisling or Cocktail
  sherry
1 teaspoon nutmeg

Combine all ingredients, mix with electric beater about 5 minutes, at medium speed. Pour batter into greased bundt cake pan and bake in 350° oven for 45 minutes or until done.

Jeani Martin pairs this quick and easy dessert with their Fountain Grove Grey Reisling for instant entertaining.

Poached Muscat Pears

2 pears, cut in half and cored, leaving a good sized hole - leave skin on
1/2 cup chopped walnuts
butter lettuce for garnish

Saute pears on both sides in small amount of butter. Add chopped walnuts, 1/2 cup Muscat wine. Cover and poach 5 minutes or until pears are still firm. Refrigerate overnight. Place pears on bed of butter lettuce, sprinkle with more walnuts and Muscat. Top with whipped cream and a cherry. Serves 4.

Jeani Martini
Martini & Prati Wines

Biscotti
(Italian Christmas Cookies)

6 eggs
2 cups sugar
3 cups sifted flour
3 teaspoons baking powder
grated lemon rind
1 1/2 cubes melted butter

1 teaspoon vanilla
2 teaspoons almond extract
1 teaspoon (or more) anise seed
1 teaspoon anise extract
1 jigger brandy
1 cup chopped almonds

Cream together eggs, sugar, flour and baking powder. Add the rest of the ingredients. Pour onto greased cookie sheet with edges. Bake at 350° for 30 to 40 minutes. Cut into serving size biscuits and place each piece on its side on cookie sheet. The biscotti will not all fit on one cookie sheet. Return to oven for a few minutes to brown slowly so they're nice and crunchy. Don't forget to toast both sides.

Perfect for dunking into Sausal Zinfandel or Cabernet.

Roselee Demostene & Cindy Martin, Co-Owners
Sausal Winery

Irish Jubilee Cake Bread

1 package date bread mix
6 ounces cream cheese
1/4 cup granulated sugar
1/2   powdered sugar
2 eggs
1 tablespoon olive oil

1 cup Eagle Ridge Sierra Jubilee
1/2 cup nuts
1/2 cup raisins
1 cup chopped dates
green food color

The night before, completely soak dates and raisins in Sierra Jubilee. Heat oven to 350°. Grease and flour a 9x5 (or so) loaf pan. In a small bowl blend cream cheese, granulated sugar and 1 egg. Beat at medium speed until smooth with 3-4 drops of green food coloring. Set aside. In a large mixer bowl, blend bread mix, 1 cup Sierra Jubilee (use the liquid from the soaked dates and raisins, add additional Sierra Jubilee to make 1 cup), 1 tablespoon oil and 1 egg until smooth. Place 1/3 of cake batter into pan and carefully spread to all corners. Then add all of the small bowl filling, again spreading carefully to all corners. Pour remaining batter on top of filling. To marble, place any knife into the pan and pull knife through batter in wide curves. Turn pan and repeat. Bake at 350° for 70 minutes (or so) or until a toothpick inserted in center comes out clean. Remove from pan.

GLAZE:

1/2 cup powdered sugar
1 tablespoon Sierra Jubilee

1 tablespoon melted cream
 cheese

Whip above ingredients until smooth. Spread or brush over cooled loaf as desired. Store in refrigerator. Serves 12.

Barry C. Lawrence, Owner & Winemaster
Eagle Ridge Winery

While it is contrary to our policy of not naming a specific brand name to a wine utilized as an ingredient, we made an exception for this wine and recipe because the wine is not a varietal or generic, but a spiced wine that is unique in its flavor and bouquet.

Lace Apples

1/4 cup Port
2 1/2 pounds tart cooking apples
(about 5 apples) peeled, cored
and cut into lengthwise slices
1/2 to 3/4 inch at thickest part
1 1/2 tablespoons fresh lemon juice
1 cup sifted all-purpose flour
1 1/2 cups sugar

1/4 teaspoon salt
1/4 teaspoon ground cinnamon
2/3 cups chopped slivered
almonds
1/2 cup melted unsalted butter
3/4 teaspoon vanilla
1 to 1 1/2 cups unsweetened
heavy cream, very softly
whipped

Pour Port over bottom of a buttered shallow dish (full 1 1/2 quart capacity). Turn apples with lemon juice to coat. Spread over Port in pan. Thoroughly stir together flour, sugar, salt, cinnamon and almonds. Mix butter and vanilla; add to almond mixture; stir with a fork until mixed and crumbly. Sprinkle evenly over apples. Bake in a 375° oven until topping is richly golden brown, about 35 to 40 minutes. Partially cool on rack. Spoon out to serve, keeping sugar mixture on top. Top generously with whipped cream. Serves 8.

Shirley Sarvis, Consulting Chef
Ficklin Vineyards

Shirley Sarvis, whose writing credits include "Gourmet," "The Time Life Cookbooks," created this recipe for Ficklin Vineyards Port Wine.

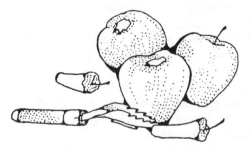

Creama Catalana

3 cups milk
peel of 1 lemon, pith removed
2 cinnamon sticks (3 inches each)

6 egg yolks
10 tablespoons sugar
3 tablespoons cornstarch

Bring milk to boil with lemon peel and cinnamon sticks; reduce heat to low. Simmer, stirring occasionally, 10 minutes. Remove cinnamon sticks and lemon peel and discard. In top of double boiler, beat egg yolks and 4 tablespoons of the sugar together until light and lemon colored; beat in cornstarch until smooth. Add 1/2 cup of the milk, stirring constantly with wooden spoon, until smooth, until custard coats a spoon, about 20 minutes. Divide custard evenly into six ovenproof dessert cups. Chill custard thoroughly, about 3 hours. Just before serving, sprinkle 1 tablespoon of remaining sugar over each serving. Set cups 4 to 5 inches away from a moderately hot broiler; broil until sugar is brown and caramelized, about 5 minutes. Serves 6.

Recommended wine: Gloria Ferrer 1986 Royal Cuvée

From Gloria Ferrer Champagne Caves

Champagne Chiffon Cake

1 cup cake flour
1 cup granulated flour
2 teaspoons baking powder
1/2 teaspoon salt
1 tablespoon corn oil

3 egg yolks
1 tablespoon lemon zest
1/2 cup Brut Champagne
5 egg whites
1/2 teaspoon cream of tartar

Mix flour, sugar, baking powder and salt together. In another bowl, combine egg yolks, oil, zest and champagne. Mix well and add flour mixture, beating until well mixed and thickened. In a clean bowl, beat egg whites with cream of tartar until stiff peaks form. Carefully pour flour mixture into egg whites. Pour batter into ungreased bundt or springform pan. Bake 35-40 minutes in 325° oven, or until cake feels springy. Glaze with a lemon glaze or serve with strawberry-rhubarb compote.

Serve with Korbel Brut Champagne.

F. Korbel & Bros., Inc.

Zucchini Zinfandel Chocolate Loaf

1 cup unsweetened cocoa
2 eggs
1/2 cup oil
1 cup sugar
2 tablespoons poppyseeds
1/2 cup milk
1 cup zucchini, shredded &
  unpeeled

1/4 cup Zinfandel
2 cups flour
1 teaspoon baking powder
1 teaspoon baking soda
1/2 teaspoon salt
1 teaspoon cinnamon
1/2 teaspoon nutmeg

Stir all ingredients together well and pour into a greased 8x5 inch loaf pan. Bake at 325° for 60 to 70 minutes.

Serve with Martinelli's Zinfandel or Muscat Alexandria.

Julie Martinelli
Martinelli Vineyards

Gewurztraminer Sorbet

4 cups water
2 cups sugar
4 teaspoon lemon juice

3/4 cup orange juice
1 bottle sweet Gewurztraminer

Boil water and sugar. Cool. Add juices and wine. Blend. Freeze overnight. Remove from freezer and beat 1 or 2 times in mixer to break up ice crystals. Refreeze until serving time. Garnish with mint, oranges or kiwi. Delicious! Makes 1/2 gallon.

Frances R. Winchell
Gan Eden Wines

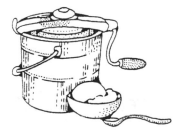

Raspberry Sorbet

1 cup water
2 pints raspberries
1 teaspoon lemon juice

2/3 cup sugar
1 egg white, lightly beaten

In large saucepan heat water and sugar to boiling, add raspberries. Transfer to food processor and puree. Strain into a large bowl and refrigerate until cold, 20 minutes. Just before freezing, whisk beaten egg white and lemon juice into the chilled puree. Freeze in an ice-cream maker according to manufacturer's directions. Makes 6 cups. 65 calories per 1/2 cup. Great color, great taste, perfect for a hot summer day.

Carol Kozlowski-Every,
From Kozlowski Farms

Cabernet Sauvignon Sorbet

2 cups Cabernet Sauvignon
1 cup granulated sugar
1 cup lemon juice

2 cups grape juice (approximately
2 pounds Flame grapes)

Combine wine and sugar in a non-corroding saucepan. Cook over medium heat until the alcohol vaporizes and the sugar is completely dissolved. Chill the wine syrup. Crush the grapes in a food processor fitted with the metal blade. Soak a double thickness of cheesecloth in water and wring dry. Into a medium size bowl, squeeze the grapes in the cheesecloth to extract the grape juice. Combine 2 cups of grape juice with 1 cup lemon juice and chill. Combine the grape-lemon juice with the wine syrup. Freeze according to the instruments with your ice cream maker. Yield: 1 quart.

Donna Kilgore
Kenwood Vineyards

Crémant Sorbet

1 1/2 cups water
2 tablespoons water
1 1/4 cup sugar
1/2 cup fresh lemon juice

zest from 1 lemon
1 cup Crémant
2 egg whites

Combine 1 1/2 cups water and 1 cup of sugar. Bring to boil, remove from heat and add lemon juice and zest. Add 1 cup Cremant and refrigerate until chilled. Dissolve 1/4 cup sugar in 2 tablespoons water. Bring to a boil and cook 1 minute. Remove from heat. Beat egg whites with wire whisk until foamy. Add hot syrup in a thin steady stream. Beat until egg whites are stiff. Stir in Champagne syrup and follow ice cream maker directions or place sorbet mixture in covered container and freeze. Serves 6 to 8.

Serve with Crémant.

Jamie Davies, Co-Owner
Schramsberg Vineyards and Cellars

INDEX
OF
RECIPES